SWITCHING GEARS

THERE ARE NO RULES

SWITCHING GEARS

THERE ARE NO RULES

Joel Walker & Terry Ainsworth

gatekeeper press™

Columbus, Ohio

Switching Gears: There Are No Rules

Published by Gatekeeper Press

2167 Stringtown Rd, Suite 109

Columbus, OH 43123-2989

www.GatekeeperPress.com

ISBN (paperback): 9781662911118

eISBN: 9781662911125

In Memoriam

As this book was headed to the publisher, Terry fell victim to COVID-19, likely contracted from having to travel every other week to Miami in order to continue the trial for Multiple Myeloma at Sylvester Cancer Center, which is attributed to him being in remission. Sadly, Terry did not survive this virus and passed away in Boone, NC on August 23, 2021.

Terry, I feel you "on my coattails", forever infusing me with your spirit and soul and love. We are whispering out loud, touching without contact, seeing without vision and reaching for you as the universe echoes your presence.

Your zest for life; your creativity; always wanting to help others and seeing the glass as half full enlightens your path. You are an amazing role model and I am proud and honored to have you as my friend.

You climbed every mountain; you are a guiding light, an inspirational force in the lives of many. I looked up the list of attributes in our book, Switching Gears, and I would check off every one for you. And, I would add one more – you are my brother.

Your friend in eternity,
Joel Walker

One of the very first things Terry instilled in me was that "Everything in life is a minor inconvenience as long as you get to keep your birthday!" I adopted and shared that philosophy with many friends, peers and employees over the next 40 years. Today, sadly, August 23, 2021, Terry lost his birthday. During what, in retrospect, seems like a short life, his lessons were inspirational and educational as he strived not only to learn something new every day but to share that learning in order to enhance another life. Terry was always curious as he searched for a better…."whatever". His honesty was unquestionable and his lessons were delivered by how he lived and thought. He experienced all of the attributes necessary to Switch Gears and he adapted to change willingly. I was honored to be called "friend", and it was both my pleasure and privilege to serve as his Editor for this and his previous book. From the notes he had shared for his 3rd book, it was going to exceed the first two. Terry's journey wasn't always easy but he traveled it with an optimistic spirit and he grew each day from new experiences. I already miss you, Terry, but know you achieved every goal you set for your Vision, Mission and Value.

Your friend and Editor,
Joyce Kronenwetter

TABLE OF CONTENTS

Terry   Joel

I have been close friends with Joel since we were in our early teens. Although we both became physicians, our paths have been both divergent but complimentary. Over the years, I have been so impressed by his compassion and caring. Joel thrives in ambiguity, which also generates his creativity. I can sense the trust people must have with how his voice makes me feel as we reflect on our long friendship. Joel is both bold and sensitive and approaches people and their challenges with innovative ideas and options that he generates as improvements and problem solving. I believe this book will provide guidance and inspiration to those who embrace his perspective – David Korn, MD, CAS

When I think of my friend, Terry Ainsworth, intention and resilience are the words that stand out to describe him. Terry's life is purposeful and this allows him to move forward no matter the challenges that come his way. His approach to life inspires all those who know him. Keep Soaring! – David McNally, Author, CPAE*

* Council of Peers Award for Excellence in Speaking

Joel is so gentle and humble and the most caring person I've ever had the pleasure to know. Only his inquisitiveness surpasses his humility. How I wish I could provide him with 2 lifetimes to satisfy his intellectual curiosity. Guy Laieta, Boxing Teacher

Terry, from the experience of knowing you for, what, 35 years or more, it was great fun to distill the essence of you down to a phrase: "Positive expectation". "Optimistic abundance" is a more twisted version. And then there's "tenacious" as well – Bailey Allard, Business Coach

Terry, you are Purposeful - in all areas of life you live on purpose, loving your family, cherishing your friends, leading your clients, and always looking for the meaning of a situation – Heather Todd

Through this time of exceptional noise, upheaval and relentless change, Joel's quiet voice is one to listen for. His respect for intuition and his enthusiasm about following it have brought him unanticipated opportunities and adventures. He has lived the choice of *Switching Gears* in his own life, and his open mind and heart draw people, both human and animal, to trust and want to be near him. He is a gentle catalyst for letting go of what in life has stopped working and takes notice of what creative voice might be calling to Switch Gears and say "Yes" to new and more fulfilling possibility – Jessica Reaske, Author, Editor

Dr. Joel Walker is one of the most genuine, caring and talented individuals that has been my privilege to know. He has combined his exceptional ability as a psychiatrist with his talent for abstract photography to develop a unique method of therapy and has taught this method to many other psychiatrists. He has written numerous articles about psychiatry and photography. He is a true Renaissance Man. Having a friend like Joel has enriched my life in many ways – Marvin Resnick

DEDICATIONS

Terry Ainsworth

One of my mom's favorite singers was Josh Groban. At her funeral, we played one of his songs that I felt spoke to who she was in my eyes. The song is entitled "You Raised Me Up". It was so fitting to her legacy. So Mom, *Switching Gears* is dedicated to you because you did "Raise Me Up". You gave me wings, values, the ability to grow and *Switch Gears* successfully. There have been many times in my youth and beyond that your experiences and teachings gave me the courage to *Switch Gears* so here's to you, MOM!

Joel Walker

My Superhero, Advocate, Cheerleader! You were my guiding light; your recognition and insight into my learning disabilities forged the way for me to succeed. You tirelessly quizzed and organized me. You were selfless and devoted. You were a gentle soul, wise and loving. You encouraged me to trust myself and to be persistent. You inspired courage in me and the spirit to overcome. You will live in my heart forever. Thank you, Mom, for giving me the gift of *Switching Gears*!

PROLOGUE

The context of *Switching Gears* is about life transitions that tie to change, which is a constant in the world today. There is at least one woman and one man in every city, county and state that either has or will *Switch Gears*, and some that may be in the midst of the transition at this moment. Their success or failure is key to their fundamental well-being. The stories we have shared may be inspirational or they may just remind you of your own experience. Some may see change as "rocking their world", while others may be excited about it, lean into it and can't wait for the next big change to happen. Then, there are those who are beleaguered and just cannot handle one more change in their life as they have already had too much. They feel terrified by change; and, therefore, are change-adverse and looking for stability. There is yet another group who choose to *Switch Gears,* and not necessarily as a result of something happening to them. It could just be spontaneity driven by impulse. An example would be someone standing in the woods who decides to become a lumberjack. Or someone working in California and decides they are bored and perhaps a move to Australia is good! Regardless of how it comes about, in order to ensure success, it will require an action plan. And, there are no rules!

Switching Gears may help you as you react to change and what you do with it when it comes your way. How you respond depends on your innate temperament and your perception of change. It will also be different based upon your age whether 20, 40, 60 or 80. Everyone brings their lifetime to each experience and all of them are different. We have shared stories of different people and experiences who have S*witched Gears* and then ask you reflective questions about those stories.

Readers of S*witching Gears* may just be curious about its meaning while others may find it to be timely for their current situation. We know many of our readers are looking for a source to comfort or help them as they realize where they are in relation to others, especially in the environment we find ourselves in today. Along with the authors of these stories, we hope that perhaps S*witching Gears* becomes an inspiration for you in learning that there can be more to life with many possibilities.

As you read each story, think of your situation and determine its relevance: What do you take away in meaning and learning? We will give you our thoughts that are in no way all encompassing. It will be our readers' perspective and meaning that will tell us if we've accomplished our purpose.

This book came about as a result of a discussion between the two authors, both of whom found that the traditional notion of "retirement" just didn't work for them and, perhaps, it doesn't even fit today's work world. As they explored this topic based on their 40 plus years of experience, one as a psychiatrist and the other an advisor to entrepreneurs, they came to the conclusion that retirement is "old school" thinking. Today, it's more about "S*witching Gears*".

"We wanted to change the paradigm to S*witching Gears*, which is defined as changing what you are doing, especially the way you think about a particular activity", said Walker and Ainsworth. There are transitional moments in a person's life when they ponder, "Perhaps my life can be richer than I have ever thought about".

Therefore, *Switching Gears* is designed to help people open their eyes to the possibilities. The range of awareness is at a different level for each person. This book provides a process to help them through a juncture in their life of not only retiring, but of being fired, dealing with death or divorce or being unfulfilled in what they are doing as well as many other examples. They must believe, trust and know that a change will take place and understand that the journey is personal for everyone. We will share stories and examine the themes behind each story to help provide an understanding of what is going on and the lessons the individuals learned as a result of the transition.

THERE ARE NO RULES

This will be exciting for some of you and absolutely terrifying for others who are *Switching Gears*. What Joel and I have learned as we wrote this book is that people who have lived in a world of being an entrepreneur, or those who think like one, have often operated outside of establishments' rules most of their lives. So it appears effortless in terms of them making transitions throughout their lives. Retirement is a rule established by someone else, and is often for those whose experience has generally been with large corporations, government, military or other establishments or institutions where there are a lot of rules and they will struggle with this notion. If that is how you think, it will affect you *Switching Gears* effortlessly.

As Joel and I sat together one morning working on this book, we talked a great deal about both of us having been rule breakers in our careers. Terry's experience, as a former banker, was filled with lots of rules for everything. And almost from the beginning of his career, he wanted out of that environment so as to be able to create what he wanted each day. So, for him, *Switching Gears* was easier because he has long had a clear Vision, Purpose, and Values that he aligned with every day. These tenets have become his guiding force that tell him if what he was switching to is on Purpose. His Vision, Mission and Values have changed. For his Vision, he wants to be known as the most admired business advisor, mentor, author, writer, husband, dad, Boppa (grandfather) and friend. For his Mission, enhancing the lives and livelihoods of all those he interacts with in his life; and, his Values are honesty, integrity, authenticity and respectability.

For Joel, his career as a psychiatrist took him on a path he least expected. Armed with years of training in different and the latest modalities, he opened his private practice. The empty walls made him feel cold and uncomfortable so, with a need to bring life to his office, he turned to his second passion, photography. His ethereal, ambiguous, dream-like abstract photographs resonated with him as he hung them – adding a familiar warmth.

"I'm terrified to go or not to go! Will I be free and fly or will I sink deeper into myself with no way out?" said a patient responding spontaneously and unprovoked to one of the photographs. Eureka! He followed her lead and explored the image in greater depth. This was the spark that led him to marry his psychiatry and photography. With this unconventional merger of passions, he found new inspirations. He shouts, "I'm alive!"

Joel became one of the earliest pioneers in PhotoTherapy using photographs as a projective to help patients verbalize, explore underlying feelings and core conflicts. Some psychiatrists and other mental health professionals are currently using these images in psychotherapy.

Photography – his passion burns deep within him, lighting his way. His first language is visual as he speaks through his evocative, surreal images using the camera as a paintbrush – it is an extension of him. The line blurs between his hand and the camera. He has become a fusion of flesh and lens; is immersed with every bit of body and soul. He instinctively knows when it is time to capture the moment. Intuitively, he created this novel technique by breaking many of the rules of photography. He is free to explore, discover, and unlock his full potential in both photography and psychiatry. Climb beyond conventional structure. Reach beyond your limitations. Create a path where no path has yet been realized. *Switch* your *Gears* freely. *Switch* truly. That next *Gear* may be the one that makes for a life you always wanted.

Today Joel has a license plate on his car that reads "**ROLWTHIT**". He has believed in this philosophy throughout his life and it has served him well. Prior to that plate, he had one that read "**2CHANCE**", which also reflects *Switching Gears*.

When you think about people like Mark Cuban, Jeff Bezos, Mark Zuckerberg, Steven Jobs, Elon Musk and Richard Branson, you'll learn that they found ways to break the rules, intentionally, to achieve their Vision and Purpose. Their actions were ethical and they did it in an entrepreneurial way. They will never retire but will *Switch Gears* many times throughout their lives.

The stories that we have shared in this book represent people who have found ways around the rules, but also includes those who have stayed within the rules of their profession. *Switching Gears* requires **trust** in yourself and letting go of those rules. You can do, think, create, build, start, reinvent and redefine your life any way you want.

Joel Walker & Terry Ainsworth

ACKNOWLEDGEMENTS

We wish to acknowledge and thank the many people that contributed to the success of this book; those who reviewed it for us and provided valuable feedback along the way:

- David McNally for his guidance, feedback and advice on writing a book.
- All of the contributors of stories within the book.
- To all the people listed below who have read edits of the book and given us valuable feedback:
  - Rebecca Lovern
  - Elysha Walker
  - Bernice Finkelstein
  - Ty DeMuynk
  - Alan Skelton
  - Jane Martin
  - Murray & Marilyn Mackenzie
  - Hal Welsh
  - Matt Manciagli
  - Bailey Allard
  - Marc Jaffee
  - Adam Walker
  - Nanci Nance
  - Max Isley

- Marnie Wedlake
- Richard Nadin
- Diane De Santis

And lastly, our wives, Bonnie Alter and Marlene Walker, who gave us time and encouragement to help us along the way. In fact, it was Marlene who, during a lunch at Storie St. Grill in Blowing Rock, NC, suggested we had so much in common that we should write a book together. So this book of stories came about at Storie St. Grill – fate?

Thank you all!

1
AN ORDINARY BOY
BECOMES AN
EXTRAORDINARY MAN

Introduction:

This story is about an individual that took his childhood suffering to drive him to where he is today. Even though he paid significant consequences for his Vision, it defines who he is. This story illustrates tenacity, persistence and a willingness to take financial and personal risk. Charles is an incredible person who lived his life to the fullest. He has been a scratch golfer, race car driver, entrepreneur, and a founder of several companies, many of which he took public. Today, at 86, he continues to be involved in a company that he took public, and continues to play golf with the same vigor. Let us introduce you to Charles. Enjoy his story of Switching Gears.

Charles' story:

I remember lying awake at night in my childhood home – a 2 bedroom/1 bath house – with each parent taking turns at night keeping the rats off of us children. I remember thinking to myself, "I don't know how but I will never be poor when I grow up". So, with only an 8th grade education and realizing I would never become President of General Motors, even though I would eventually achieve more, I set out to make my Vision a reality.

After leaving school, I felt I only had two choices if I was going to achieve my goal of being wealthy. The first was to go into sales and the second was to own my own business. I sold everything from freezers to bronzed baby shoes. After serving our country, I returned home with a 15-year old wife and took a job paying me $0.75 an hour or $28.12 a week net take-home pay. I had a child on the way and we were buying a home, the price of which was $4,900 with a monthly payment of $28. It was financed by the GI Bill.

I was soon introduced to a business that sold food to stock a freezer which the customer purchased from the company and which was delivered to the customers' homes. I earned $300 my first night selling to four neighbors who became my first customers. I stayed with that job until I was offered a position as Plant Manager that paid $8,000 per year. Later, I left that job to become Assistant to the President of an electric supply company. Then I was offered a position with a lighting manufacturer as Vice President and potential stock ownership. When the stock ownership did not come through, I quit, even without another job, and I started my own business as a Manufacturer's Representative. This company became the umbrella for all my future businesses. As the business grew and I needed capital to take it to the next level, I researched taking the company public and first did so in 1967 raising $300,000. There were multiple companies along the way that I took public so I knew I had found my strategy to becoming rich.

My expertise in taking a company public grew and so did my knowledge as I read and researched on my own. Eventually, I came to know more about this process than some of the bankers and venture capitalists I knew in the business. The niche I established was in the electrical supply component, lighting and wire industry. However, along the way, I also owned other companies, one which grew to become the largest video duplication business.

Two of the most important lessons I learned was to take a chance and also to take stock rather than cash. An example was one of the companies I worked with gave me the choice of $15,000 cash, 15% ownership in the company or $15,000 worth of stock. I chose the stock which turned into $1,500,000. I never doubted being successful. I had built a good network of people that grew over time, and I was an avid reader and a member of YPO (Young Presidents' Organization) for many years. My only regret was that I missed seeing my daughters grow up; however, over time, I came to have a wonderful relationship with them. I was married several times as a result of my pursuit to achieve my vision. In a seven year timeframe, I never missed a day for illness nor ever took a single day off for vacation. It was non-stop work which caused its consequences.

Today at 86, I continue to work-out 3 days a week with a trainer, a chiropractor and an acupuncturist. I am still working, involved on several boards and loving it. I have achieved my goal of a consummate entrepreneur with a Vision of never being poor, a Mission of making each situation better than it previously was, whether personal or business, and have learned a strategy to accomplish both.

One of my success stories is of a company whose sales went from $10 million to $30 million, then to $70 million, and today doing $1 billion in sales with $100,000 million in cash, no debt and 2 million square feet of warehouse. It trades on the NASDAQ and I continue to serve on its Board.

Switching Gears has been natural for me because I always knew what my end goal was. As long as the move was in line with what I wanted to achieve, then it was the right thing to do. My word was my bond and I have always taken care of my family and treated people fairly. A life well lived where luck meets opportunity and owning was and is the key strategy.

Authors' Thoughts:

This is a linear progression of *Switching Gears*. As we interviewed and compiled Charles' story, the attributes of education, ethics, commitment, persistence and a belief system that reinforces thriving, tenacity, confidence resonated loud and clear about Charles' life and *Switching Gears*. He clearly had a Vision to never be poor, only wealthy. Every step he took, every job he had and every decision he made was clearly in line with accomplishing that Vision. He was confident, never had a fear of failing, and took chances by giving up cash for stock, something most people would not choose to do. To this day, this is who Charles is. Oh, and by the way, in the midst of this life, he was a race car driver and a single digit handicapper!

Reflections:

_____

Sometimes there are negative consequences for achieving your goals. As we reflect on Charles' story, it's painful to hear of his sacrifices but his choices were in line with his Vision.

- As you read Charles' story, what were you thinking about relative to your life? What of his story was not relative to you?

- What was your vision of what you wanted to be when you grew up? Didn't have one. Why? If you did have one, have you achieved it and why?

- What were Charles' strengths and weaknesses? What did he do to overcome his weaknesses? Think about yours and what have you done to improve so as to _Switch Gears_?

Teaching Point:

Know what you don't want.

Life is not measured by the number of breaths you take but by the moments that take your breath away.

Determine to live life with flair and laughter.

Maya Angelou

2
BEING A PATIENT
REQUIRES PATIENCE

Terry 2020 healthy with Multiple Myeloma

Patience is that virtue that teaches us no matter how
life surprises us, the good and not so good, we have the
ability, the capacity and the spirit to handle it.

David McNally, Author, "Mark Of An Eagle"

Introduction:

Being a patient in a hospital requires patience, different but the same as does Switching Gears. What did Terry learn? First, trust the process and, secondly, believe in doctors. In his story, he shares with you what he means and how it will tie directly to Switching Gears.

Terry's story:

In early September of 2016, Bonnie and I were on a cruise to Italy where we kayaked on the Croatia River and I, purposefully, decided to go over a 9' waterfall in my kayak. We toured Sorrento, the Amalfi Coast, and ate in "The Blue", our favorite restaurant on the ship that was a hike from our room every day and night. Full out enjoying every experience – we walked the streets of Venice, took a water taxi to and from the hotel and, finally, boarded a plane for the 16-17 hour trip home.

I tell you this because not long after we returned to our "normal" life, I began experiencing some of the pain that had first begun in October and, after a couple of trips to my chiropractor, I received the diagnosis of possibly a "floating rib" fracture, but nothing significant or anything of any real concern. All seemed to go well until December, and as I was sitting in a chair in our bedroom, I sneezed and immediately experienced some excruciating pain. I managed to get another appointment right away with my chiropractor who, once again, made an adjustment that brought some minor relief.

Then, on January 5, 2017, we left for our scheduled drive to Florida where we typically spend the winter. And, as is usual, we began by driving to Charlotte for the night and then on to Weston, FL the following day. I typically drive the entire trip to Florida, but I seemed to feel tired, and so Bonnie relieved me for about an hour while I took a break and then I finished the remainder of the drive. Prior to leaving the NC mountains, we had been in touch with my college roommate, Ty, who was battling cancer, and we had scheduled to have lunch with him and his wife, Cheryl, on our way south. However, as it turned out, on the day we were going to be in their area, Ty was scheduled for a treatment of radiation, chemo and his doctor's appointment so we had to cancel our lunch. Little did we know how significant this routine would become to us not too far in the future. So, rather than stop for lunch, we continued on to Florida and arrived in Weston in the late afternoon, had a nice drink and ate dinner in the condo.

Throughout the rest of January, I continued to experience a lot of pain, but we continued our life, having dinner with friends, going to the Club, golf for Bonnie although none for me. Getting in and out of bed had become very painful. Then, later in the month, on January 23rd, we were scheduled to have dinner with friends but it turned out I wasn't feeling well so we cancelled. We had been so looking forward to it but I just didn't think I could do it.

The following day, I went to the ER for x-rays that revealed I had two broken ribs. Nothing could be done. Just a couple of days later, the 26th, at the recommendation of an orthopedic surgeon/ friend, we went back to the ER where they performed a CT scan. The next morning, Friday, as we were having breakfast with Honey King & Ken Carpenter at Offerdahl Café, I received a call from Dr. Russell's practice informing me I had an appointment with Dr. Al Maaieh at the University of Miami Hospital on the following

Tuesday, January 31. I was told the CT scan showed multiple lytic lesions in my back and the preliminary diagnosis was **Multiple Myeloma**. It was on this DAY and at this MOMENT when my world stopped turning. I had just been diagnosed with a disease that attacks the bone marrow. Indications were I had multiple lesions not only in my back, but in my legs, spine, and shoulder – just about everywhere! No wonder I was in such pain. OMG –

I

HAVE

CANCER!!

Of course, off to Google I go – reading, researching Multiple Myeloma. What is it? What is the prognosis? What is the treatment? What kind of life will I have? Talk about *Switching Gears!*

So many questions…..

How long have I had it?

What is the cause?

Are my children at risk?

It is treatable, not curable – what does that mean?

Time frame from initial pain to diagnosis October 17 to January 27 – 15 weeks – 3.7 months!

I recalled that Alan Jackson wrote a song after 9/11 titled, "*Where Were You When the World Stopped Turning*". That song now has a special meaning to me and that day – January 27. The beginning of this story gives one an indication of what our lives were prior to this date. I recall a young social worker we met, Adrienne, an oncologist concierge, was in my room one day and during our conversation asked me the question - "What was your life like before Multiple Myeloma?" Bonnie and I just looked at each other and laughed. My answer was full out as the illustrations reflect.

The next few days are a blur but the BIG appointment was with Dr. Al Maaieh, which would be the beginning of a special relationship. Then on to meet my Multiple Myeloma doctor, Dr. James Hoffman. Both of these doctors asked us, "How did you get to us?" We didn't know – God, I guess. They are the best of the best - the competencies of these two doctors gave me great comfort that the prognosis was going forward. Thinking back now, I know we got to both of them through Ben Riestra, President of The Lennar Foundation Medical Center who is a best friend of Bonnie's daughter, Ashley, and great friends with Tom Brady, our son-in-law. It seems it still boils down to who you know, or who they know – in a good way.

Being admitted to a hospital is one thing, but actually getting into a hospital is another – and quite an adventure. Another illustration that "being a patient requires patience"! Going there for my bone marrow biopsy was a comedy of errors. First, when we arrived at the University of Miami Hospital, we were told we were supposed to be at the Sylvester Center – across the street. For the trip, I had been forced to lie in the back seat of our car where I could be the most comfortable. Thank God I had not gotten out of the car right away. The valet was kind enough to say "no charge" for parking! Next, we drove over to Sylvester Center and pulled up to the front entrance only to find out we needed to be at the rear. Mind you, I'm still lying in the back seat of the car, in excruciating pain, with Bonnie crying her eyes out because we felt so helpless. Then I finally did have to get out of the car – still in severe pain and saying to everyone, "No one can touch me" – to get into a wheelchair.

Of course, by this time, Bonnie was practically hysterical. We go to the 2nd floor – "In-Patient". By this time, I'm in so much pain I literally cannot move. We are directed to Dr. Hoffman's floor only to learn that we really did need to be at the University of Miami Hospital – where we had just come from! This time, they said they were going to call for an ambulance to transport me. But, when we were told it was going to take 1½ hours to get to me, I said, "No, let's go on our own – I can endure the pain one more time to be at the right place". Down the elevator – a valet gets our car – and, once again, I crawled into the back seat, still in pain, but into a position that contained it.

Back over to the University of Miami Hospital, through another toll gate, to the ER entrance to meet up with Jose. However, there was no Jose at ER entrance. We were directed to go back to the front of the hospital where, we're told, "He's waiting with a wheelchair". During all of this, I'm trying to console Bonnie – by now she has reached full blown hysteria. As we pull up to the front of the hospital, and after valet parking, Bonnie goes to look for Jose just as we see him exit and _give MY wheelchair to someone else!_ Then he noticed Bonnie and asked her if I was her husband, to which she says, "Yes". He apologizes for giving my wheelchair away, goes to find another one and finally comes to the car where I'm still lying, fairly comfortably, with the windows down and a nice breeze keeping me cool. After some time, I'm able to get out of the car and into a wheelchair – I'm still in tremendous pain. We go through the preliminary check-in – still such a hassle – and then Jose takes me to the room that had been reserved for me on the 8th floor – Oncology. Little did I know that this room would become my home for the next 16 days – I would not be leaving for a while! The date was February 5th.

This entire experience required copious amounts of patience as I was required to *Switch Gears* several times every day. My life had been disrupted. Things that were important before became insignificant. I had to be patient waiting for tests, then procedures, then results, not to mention waiting for doctors, nurses, X-rays, MRI's and everything else you expect when in the hospital. For me, this was the biggest event since (my first wife) Susan's death and it forced me to *Switch Gears* constantly. I think that as you process all the stories in our book, you will see elements of being patient in the process.

A key attribute for me is a wholehearted belief in my doctors and Sylvester Cancer Center. If I didn't have that belief, there would have been a direct effect on all my other attributes. I have had the belief from the beginning that I am going to beat this disease and still believe that to this day, especially knowing that they're more treatments being created as we go to press. My most recent treatment of Darzalex is an example of that. The fact that I will be able to take my treatment subcutaneously within the next year helps me maintain that attitude. I have also learned to have compassion for people whose lives are disrupted with the diagnosis of cancer. When you hear those three words – "YOU HAVE CANCER" – you are struck with real fear – terror! That phrase hits you like no other. If you have the attitude of beating cancer, you must be courageous because there will be numerous times when you will experience setbacks, delays, reactions, emotional relapses and many other unforeseen outcomes. Courage is something you will see daily as you sit in infusion rooms with many other people who are fighting this disease along with you.

Another attribute that I developed is the willingness to gain more knowledge about my disease and its many possible directions. I didn't have a clue what Multiple Myeloma was when I was first diagnosed but, since then, I have immersed myself with learning as much as I can. Humility is a trait that you develop as you deal with cancer. In the beginning, I didn't want anyone to know; I was self-conscious how I looked and thought. But, today, I'm like an open book and comfortable with people knowing that I have Multiple Myeloma and am doing quite well, thank you very much! I have learned to *Switch Gears* throughout my journey, adopting new attributes of leaning or calling on others to get me through what life has to offer. Let me say here that you don't get through a battle with cancer without faith, family and friends. You find out who your true friends are and those who are not. People will come out of the woodwork that you never thought would and others will hide. I have a new friend, Rob Lacy, the son-in-law of our friends, Charlie and Joyce Harris. Rob is younger than me, has Multiple Myeloma and has been through stem cell transplant. He has been in remission since April of 2020. We have talked numerous times about our experiences and he has guided me to many articles and webinars on our disease. An example of a friend unbeknownst to me prior to Multiple Myeloma.

I could go on writing for some time as my journey continues. As of November, 2020, I am waiting to learn if I will be accepted into a clinical trial that could potentially put me in remission, a word that hasn't been used up to this point. It is again requiring patience, trust in my doctor and the process. Easy to say – VERY hard to do. I've had to *Switch Gears* again, but in this case, it could "enhance" my life <u>forever</u>.

Authors' Thoughts:

My journey is not over. I have learned new attributes such as "flexibility" and new coping skills to help me deal with the roller coaster of emotions of having patience.

Reflections:

- What has happened in your life to test your patience? Was it a catastrophic event?

- What were you thinking about while reading Terry's story?

- What kept Terry from becoming immobile, stuck, angry, cynical and unable to *Switch Gears*?

Teaching Point:

Be a symbol of hope; I've got too much music left in me.

3
IT'S NEVER TOO LATE TO FIND YOUR PASSION
Part I

Introduction:

From a government employee to wildlife photographer, Jack has faced his fears, embraced his passion and is Switching Gears to be true to himself. You can feel the energy and emotion in his intimate portrayals. He is an outstanding teacher who is definitely in his element and now wears a smile from ear to ear.

Jack's story:

For 24 years, I have died a thousand deaths, full of sadness and emptiness and feeling unfulfilled. I was glued to a desk every day, in a government job; wondering if my talents and passions would ever be exploited. I thought, "In 4 more years, at age 55, I can retire with a pension". I had been brought up with the notion that you must work at a job that provided benefits and a pension and, while my current employment provides those, it does not stimulate me nor does it let me get in touch with my true passions.

With the government, I had the opportunity to take a sabbatical – one year off – and then return to work at the same level. The idea of that excites me and, at the same time, riddles me with fear. Can I compete with the best by pursuing my photographic nature tour business and still make a living - can I financially *Switch Gears*? I strongly believe that fear is both a natural thing and a good thing because it helps you develop courage and grit; however, you must not let it immobilize you because fear is just a feeling and it will pass.

My hunger and thirst for nature has always been a focus throughout my entire life. My heartbeat and nature are one. Since my early teens, I have had a fascination and love for marine biology, exploring the night skies with my telescope, and, more recently, photographing birds and other animals, capturing some during their migration. When I combine my love of photography with my passion for wildlife, I have a feeling similar to winning the lottery.

Self-taught in photography, I began sharing my passion for nature on-line. A foreign viewer asked if he could come and photograph with me. This individual convinced me to start a photographic business and, through this new beginning, I have made many important contacts all over the world. I was learning the business and improving my photography. Being with nature frees my soul. I feel alive, energized and serene all at the same time.

Today, I am capturing a diverse range of imagery, specializing in wildlife photography tours and workshops. I believe I capture the essence of my subjects.

Authors' Thoughts

Fear is good. It develops courage and grit, enabling you to pursue your passion. Finding, embracing and sharing it energizes you and others. This a story of hope; it's about following your heart. Jack sacrifices a lot but he never gave up.

Reflections:

- What is you belief system about your work, life and purpose? Has it been defined by others? If so, why and how?

- What is your passion and are you living it? What obstacles or beliefs are preventing you from pursuing it? Why?

- What do you think about when you hear the word "fear?

<u>Teaching Point</u>:

Be true to yourself; don't let fear have a place.

4
IT'S NEVER TOO LATE TO FIND YOUR PASSION
Part II

Jenny

Introduction:

This is a story of a young woman who took a leap of faith by beginning to train to become a triathlon athlete following meeting someone on an airplane who encouraged her to take the jump. She invited Jenny to a local triathlon club meeting and, after that meeting, Jenny began setting her training and race goals. She has always been very athletic, in great physical shape, and believed she could master this sport. She did!

Jenny's story:

I am a driven individual in all that I do. I work for a Fortune 500 company and excel in the world of sales. As a triathlon athlete, I strive to be at the highest level. Every day requires me to *Switch Gears*, especially going from work to my passion of biking, swimming and running. Talk about *Switching Gears*, it is so represented in this sport!

Beginning the swim, where I've had to battle many bodies to reach a point where I can lead the pack, then *Switching Gears* and transitioning to the bike ride, I must go from wet to dry, barefoot to bike riding shoes and helmet. All the while, I'm being clocked from the time I get on the bike to riding for miles. Once, in a race in Kona, the bike part was 25 miles; then back to the transitioning station, changing into my running shoes and off for a half marathon or more. The entire event takes hours to complete and my body was physically and mentally exhausted, but I was euphoric when I won my first race.

I had raced for a year and had come in 6th so, when I won that first race, it was my greatest accomplishment. I had worked hard for that victory, studying the times I would need to win, running up the hilly Santa Monica Mountains to get stronger. When I won, I was very emotional, tearing up and smiling from ear to ear. I was so excited - winning is the greatest feeling in competition. I had accomplished my major goal.

So how did I go from that to riding a pony and advancing a hard, white ball with a mallet 100 yards on the back of a spirited, agile and quick horse? How did I make the switch? It demanded focus, physical endurance and pushing fear aside, which exists in both sports. I trained every day, went to chukka workshops, and bought 4 horses, which you must have in a match. There are 4 15-minute chukkas and the horses are worn out after each one. I must walk and train these horses on a daily basis – as they are athletes, too – while still holding down a full-time job. It requires a tremendous amount of dedication and the ability to *Switch Gears*.

Do I find it difficult to compete in a male dominated sport? I had to stand my ground whether it's swimming in a triathlon or riding against an opposing team in polo. I don't look tough so I enjoy proving my toughness in sports. My goal was to move from a "B" rating or "-1" to a lower rating that works in favor of the team. Today, I have moved from a "-1" handicap to a "0", which means I have reached my goal. I play with professionals who are much better than I am so I have to show that I possess both the mental and physical toughness to be on that polo field. When I do that, I earn the respect and admiration of my team mates and competitors. I now own 9 horses, go to Santa Barbara every polo season and thrive at my passion. I created my own team and I launched a product line with the same name. I am continuously *Switching Gears* and living my dream!

Authors' Thoughts:

Jenny's strongest attributes that we see are determination and resilience. She has enormous belief in herself and when she puts her mind to it, she can accomplish anything. She has heart and you can see it come through in all that she does. Doing well in a male dominated sport reflects on each of these attributes. She is intelligent beyond her college education and learns what she needs to in order to succeed in the endeavor she is pursuing. Passion is instilled in her, especially when it comes to horses, dogs and all other animals – they are a major part of her life. *Switching Gears* and living her dream is what her life is all about.

Reflections:

What attributes do you see in Jenny that have enabled her to successfully Switch Gears?

- What is Jenny's tolerance for change? Is this like you or different? In what ways?

- What did you take away from this story that resonates with you?

Teaching Point:

Have the drive that underlines the ability to *Switch Gears,* focus, and have the endurance to push away fear.

5
ROLL WITH IT

Introduction:

This is a story of an amazing friend and co-author. His story is similar to the picture of the humpback whale and you'll experience the title throughout his story. Let me introduce you to Joel Walker.

Joel's story:

WOW!! I feel so alive in this moment photographing one of the most awesome beings in nature – a 66,000 pound humpback whale breaching in the Antarctic. I can identify with its spontaneity, explosive energy, unbridled creativity and playfulness. This majestic creature is, to me, the epitome of freedom; a frolicking acrobat suddenly erupting skyward from the ocean, suspended for an instant, rolling and crashing down....possibly messaging to his pod mates.

Having a philosophy or perspective on life helped me surmount barriers and encourages me to "Roll with It", or S*witch* G*ears*. My heartfelt core belief is that age is only a number; then trumpeting to the world, "I can do it!" My all potent and captivating belief – "We have the capacity to do much more with our lives than we ever thought possible" – creates and invites endless opportunities.

My passionate good-bye belief is we are all made up of different parts, and, in life, it's important to go out there and explore them. You know what guys? "It's my turn!" These were my parting words as I closed my practice. It was a heartfelt message to my patients and myself. I was giving them permission to break loose and step outside their comfort zone and go for it. Today, after that **G**ear **S**witch, I am immersed in a number of different projects. Being open, spontaneous and going with the flow energizes and lifts me to peak experiences like Maslow's state of self-actualization. An adventurer bar none, poised to ascend every mountaintop, uncluttered by danger, spirited by the call of the wild.

My license plate reads "ROLWTHIT" and I often get a "thumbs up" sign when people cross the street in front of my car. I smile. This is the motto I live by. I've always believed life has a way of giving you signs - you just have to notice. Be on the lookout, be more aware and mindful, stay in the moment and go through the doors of not knowing. The more I trust the signs, I smile to myself and say, "Here we go again". The more the signs appear, I feel as if the universe is speaking to me. These inklings or signs or "aha moments" began appearing to me when I was 12 years old. Around then, I remember seeing an airplane flying and something inside of me said it was going to crash and, within seconds, IT DID!

Prior to closing my practice and *Switching Gears*, photographic imagery had long been a large part of my life for years. I discovered the power of photographs in therapy and pioneered a treatment method known as "The Walker Visuals" where I used photographs in my practice and in workshops for more than 35 years. So it's not surprising that many of my adventures are with a camera.

One day while I was sitting at my computer, an internet ad leaped out at me and I caught the wording, "Be able to gallop out of trouble!!" It spoke of ten days on the back of a horse in the Okavango Delta, Botswana. Although I had ridden horses since I was six years old, a friend of mine who taught riding for the Royal Canadian Mounted Police Musical Ride, said to me, "I don't care how well you think you can ride, this is a real challenge for which you are not yet prepared". So, to prepare myself, for 4 months, twice a week, I worked with an instructor who had me stand in the stirrups, sometimes with a lead line, as I circled around her, first learning to balance while standing and then standing with a camera in one hand and the reins in the other as we walked, trotted, cantered and galloped. I felt like a high-wire performer in the circus with no net below me. I was eventually able to hang off the side of my horse with a wide angle lens and capture giraffes spreading out in front of me. I was able to hold my telephoto lens still as an elephant charged at me. I was also the oldest rider by 20+ years, and one of the few who never fell off the horse. I felt so proud that I was able to change a roll of film at a gallop! I always find it best to go on an adventure with no expectations; thus my mind is fully open to receive whatever the universe sends.

While talking on the phone one day, with the TV on in the background, another "aha moment" occurred as I found myself transfixed to the screen where, staring up at me, was Satu, a 2-month old Sumatram tiger cub who was to be introduced to the public at the zoo in Miami. (See picture in Chapter 10.) I was immediately enraptured by the curious, playful and mischievous nature of this youngster and knew I was destined to photograph him and help to save an endangered tiger. I grabbed my camera, headed to the zoo and, regardless of the weather, stayed for hours.

Knowing of my passion for this cub, my daughter, realizing that my 75th birthday was just around the corner, wondered what would be a meaningful gift for me. Being a good detective herself, she began researching wildlife photographers and soon found someone that she felt would be a match – Chris Weston – someone whose own photography exhibited the same sensitivity to these animals that I had. Soon thereafter, she contacted him and then left it up to the two of us to make whatever arrangements were needed to head to India to see the Bengal tigers. Before I left, I had been having some difficulty with balance as well as numbness, tingling and pain in my left leg – symptoms of sciatica. Miraculously, the trip was therapeutic. I had no time to focus on my body while bounding around in our jeep 14 hours a day, or suddenly feeling like I was going to slide off the back of our pachyderm. Interestingly, I had zero symptoms of Sciatica in India and have had absolutely none since. I guess the cure is to buy an elephant! For 6 days, in the sweltering heat of 100 degrees Fahrenheit, with dust and black soot in my nostrils, my throat, on my face and covering my cameras, I hurdled down twisting, bumpy, dirt roads in a Jeep with a naturalist who had a heavy foot, and I hung on for dear life to prevent being air-borne or catapulted into orbit.

My trip to Bandhavgarth National Park in India to photograph the Royal Bengal Tiger was life altering. I felt invigorated, in awe and mesmerized; all of my senses were heightened, primed and I was totally in the moment. I've never felt more alive in my life. This is the epitome of a life altering experience. Prior to my trip, I had imagined trying to hand-hold a long, heavy lens and camera still as I'm sliding back and forth on this gentle giant as he climbs up and down the rocky, forested floor under the canopy and at the same time keep the tigers' whiskers razor sharp and in focus.

While preparing for these encounters with nature, and along with my daughter's encouragement, at the strike of dawn, for 6 months without a miss, I emerge into the training room and transform myself into the man of steel by learning to box. My burning desire to continuously throw jabs, hooks, uppercuts as

I dance around my boxing coach. My art teacher fosters my raw talent to create impressionistic imagery with an acrylic palate. My reining quarter horse, Remi, loping and jogging, churns the dust in the arena as I learn the subtle cues to communicate with an experienced mount. I love preparing for and following up these activities so they become engraved in my mind and body. We spend 4½ to 5 months each year in the 85+ degree sunny weather of Florida which invigorates, energizes and awakens me. Bathing in the heat charges my batteries! At the end of this time, each year, I dread going back to Toronto. I am overwhelmed with feelings of loneliness, despair and trepidation; counting down the last days, having to leave but not wanting to. What's preventing me from rolling with it? I'm aghast at how difficult and overly focused I feel. What am I going to lose versus what will I gain by returning home? Do I want to return to frigid weather without the anticipation of constant activity; the lure of forever challenging myself? I realize it's not about the place but how you deal with it.

My mantra, ROLL WITH IT means to be open to possibilities – open to *Switching Gears.*

Conclusion:

Transformative encounters will spontaneously occur illuminating my path if I am open, stay positive and go with the flow. Take a risk and the rewards will be unimaginable! Great treasures lie behind the doors of not knowing. Be one with the universe; feel the ethereal, resonate with the cosmos, whisper loudly and my inner voice will be heard. Venture forth unbridled by expectations and judgements. Gliding on the wings of the wind forever spells freedom when my mind is without conscious thought. Live in the moment. Trust in the moment. Believe in the moment and just BE!

Authors' Thoughts:

Roll With It!

My philosophy of life and personal mantra acts as my compass and guide in helping me navigate through rough and calm waters. It also helps me be open to step through doors of not knowing, to discover that we are capable of much more than we ever thought.

Reflections:

- How easy or difficult would it be for you to adopt "roll with it" as your life's mantra? Why?

- What stories do you have where you were challenged?

- What's your version of a life altering event?

- What was your thinking (positive or negative self-talk) as you read Joel's adventures?

Teaching Point:

Have a philosophy and belief system. Live life to its fullest; don't wait!

6

THE RISE OF THE PHOENIX

The sad thing is that, even though we know our lives aren't working in certain areas, we are still afraid to change. We are locked into our comfort zone, no matter how self-destructive it may be. Yet, the only way to get out of that comfort zone and to be free of our problems and limitations is to get uncomfortable.

Dr. Robert Anthony, _Beyond Positive Thinking_
(30th Anniversary Edition 2018)

Introduction:

Should we expect every change in our lives to be positive? Is every Gear Switch a progression to something at a level higher than where we are at the present? Much like the transmission on a car, sometimes it will shift into a higher gear, only to find that we need more "torque" to overcome a new obstacle. Sometimes "down shifting" to generate some power is just what's needed to get us to that next level. However, unlike a car's transmission, life has lateral shifts that allow us to track an entirely new path. Here is a story about a man who Switched Gears, only to find that it wasn't the right Switch for him. Unbeknownst to him, this ill-fated maneuver would propel him into new endeavors – opening his eyes to his true passions, leading to new opportunities, and showing he was capable of more than he imagined. You might say he had to go forward, then go back.....to go forward again! Even when life takes you down a path, despite your best intentions and optimism, you may not find what you are looking for. This is never the time to give up, but rather to learn, evaluate, and grow. You are the master of your "life's gears". You can shift in all directions.

Tony's story:

I am going to die. It is the inescapable end that we all must face. I find myself lying awake, sweat dripping from my forehead. My body is hot. The hour is late. My heart pounds with so much force that I can feel a rhythmic pressure in my ears, vibrating like the taught animal skin head of a shaman's drum. I am aware in this moment that I will one day experience what it's like to die. I try to catch my breath, but the more I think about this, the more vigorous my breathing gets. I am going to die. I am 6 years old.

From an early age I have been afraid of death. Knowing this, I have taken an interest, at a young age, in learning as much as I could about the universe. I wanted to know the answers to the big questions. Why am I here? What's the purpose of everything or anything? If there is a God, who made him? Perhaps the question I most wanted answered is: Why is there anything at all? Why even the possibility for any type of existence in the first place? As I grew, I spent much of my time pondering these questions. I was convinced, early on, that if I could figure out the universe, consciousness, and my place within the universe, I could escape it at my time of death. I could find a way out of the "tunnel" I would travel down on my way to the afterlife. My error, unbeknownst to me at the time, was in my perception and my lack of understanding about many things. I had made assumptions about the universe that were incorrect, as I did about consciousness, and the potential of an afterlife. My assumptions were a product of both ignorance and credulity.

In time, I would come to idolize figures like Stephen Hawking, Roger Penrose and Richard Feynman (to name a select few) as I increased my knowledge of the cosmos. I also became fascinated with quantum physics – learning about the smallest, most fundamental components of reality. It helped me to see the world much differently. Today I make it a point to wake up and listen to a lecture on physics almost every day. Whether it's Leonard Susskind talking about the potential of a "holographic universe" or Brian Greene explaining how time is an illusion, I find myself deeply intrigued and interested. Moreover, I have developed a love of studying ancient philosophers such as Democritus, Lucretius, Plato, Socrates, etc. Rationalism and empiricism have become the standard by which I evaluate my reality. I like to think of myself today as a modern Renaissance man – although I admit that is my opinion of me and not necessarily recognized by others.

One of the hardest things I have learned to do – and I would imagine this is true for most people – is to accept reality on reality's terms, especially when it challenges what we want to believe. From where I sit now, I can safely say that Thomas Gray was right when he wrote "ignorance is bliss." For once you know the truth, it can never be unknown.

Until my early 30's, life felt "safe" to me. It was going as well as I would have expected it would, but I always felt like I had time (evidence yet again of a younger, more delusional me). It was during this time that I would be tested in many ways as I developed an intestinal illness. What began with an episode of intussusception of the intestine (a telescoping of the intestine causing a blockage) would come to rob me of nearly 2 years of my life as I dealt with intermittent abdominal pain and nausea. To this day, despite the best efforts of an amazing doctor and a "running through the gambit" of medical **diagnostic** procedures, no formal diagnosis has ever been given. The longer I went undiagnosed, the further I fell into a depression. With fear and hopelessness, I moved quickly from acquaintances to intimate friends. My fate felt out of my hands. My control was lost. Would I have to live the rest of my life in this hell – nauseous and pain stricken? I can't live like this. Death begins to look like a welcomed alternative to life when you are in pain. My illness served as a harsh reminder that I am not infallible – that my time is limited. As children, most of us view serious illness and even death as something that "happens way down the road". It feels like a place you will never get to – until you get to it. Then it feels all too real. You are constantly reminded that you are not invincible. Your mortality is overt. Another delusion lost to the experience of life. It's both a humbling and perspective altering. Fortunately for me, post laparoscopic surgery, my illness has subsided. I still live with the fear that, at any point in my life, this unknown condition could start up all over again. I don't know what I would do if that were to happen. I don't think I could go through that again.

Before my illness, I was someone else. My experiences have changed me. I juxtapose the two versions of Tony – the Tony before my illness and the one after my illness and I don't fully recognize myself. I have transitioned from delusional to verity; from credulous to skeptical. And now, at the time of this writing, I find myself transitioning yet again, from skeptical to cynical. What I've learned is to be a self-sufficient, fact-seeking person – to research and accurately interpret the information presented without bias, and portion my actions to the evidence. Philosopher Dave Hume said it best when he stated that "a wise man portions his beliefs to the evidence." I no longer recognize myself. I can only reflect on who I once was, and I honestly don't know how I feel about my former self. I am without opinion on that person. What has taken its place is something new, and yet still in transition. With each experience, I develop a more refined identity. My *Switching Gears* has been most evident when referencing the before and after me of my intestinal illness, but I have come to see that I made smaller *Gear Switches* throughout my life.

I spent my high school days dreaming of being a pediatric cardio-thoracic surgeon, but my self-imposed pressure of getting into select Ivy League medical schools left me doubtful of my capabilities. I defeated myself without even taking a chance. With the prospect of taking the MCAT test, I found comfort in giving up and switching into an entirely different career direction. I left the pre-medical/biological course of study in favor of a degree in business/management. I never felt right as a business major. I never felt like myself. I felt as if a small part of me died after leaving biology. This was further confirmed as my career moving forward, post-college, would leave me rather miserable and unsatisfied. Even after I was given the chance, years later, to go back to school and work on a post baccalaureate in biology, I still couldn't bring myself to go through with it. My fear of failure closed that door for me forever. To this day, I still retain a letter of recommendation to the U-Conn post baccalaureate program written for me by a brilliant medical doctor (and Yale clinical professor). I guess it's what I hold on to as a reminder of who I could have been. Hey, sometimes you *Switch* **Gears** for the better, and sometimes it ends up being for the worse. What matters is what you choose to do with that.

It's been a long time since the days of my college graduation. I've held a few different positions at a few different companies over the last 20 years. For the last 3 years, I've run my own fitness business and it still doesn't "feel like me." It's been a series of pitfalls almost from the start and despite my best efforts, I feel like it is just not enough. It has certainly shaken my self-confidence. I truly believed I made an intelligent decision in starting a gym, as fitness was once my passion. Please allow me to be so bold as to offer an alternative to "turn your passion into a career." I attempted to do just that, and it left me feeling like I "turned my passion into a job." My passion was better left as a personal pursuit. Now I feel trapped in a business for which I no longer have passion – waking up each morning only to find myself stagnant. Three years in, and I'm in the same place in many facets of my professional life. I feel the anxiety and anger welling up in me each day. I ride an emotional rollercoaster, constantly. I feel like I am ready to ignite.

Is it time to *Switch* **Gears** again? At this very moment, as I am writing this, that is the very question I am pondering. I'm tired of the "trial and error" method of living. I am unaware of what's to come next. It's hard to figure out who you are in a convoluted world where everything seems half-assed and backwards. I see a rat race that I don't want to be a part of anymore. Through my aforementioned newfound self-sufficiency, along with my openness to change, I may try my hand in craftsmanship as a potential career in the future. I've found a fascination with the craftsman hands. I find a calmness though watching the leatherworker handcraft a beautiful gentleman's billfold. I find pleasure in watching the woodworker craft a table or chair from raw lumber to a functional piece of "art." I have already begun this new venture by recently handcrafting décor pieces for my fitness club. With no formal training, I am free to create novel approaches to my craft. There is true satisfaction to be found in creating something with your hands from scratch. You take a unique pride in this kind of work. If satisfaction is the goal, then this may be my means to that goal.

No one says you must stay in your current gear. Life doesn't come with a rule book. When you are ready, shift into a "new gear." In saying that, I realize that the words can flow much more easily than the actions can. Saying you can *Switch Gears and* act on it may feel worlds apart despite their connection. Perhaps I am reborn – still smoldering from the ashes. Perhaps I am new. Whether for better or for worse, I know that I have forever been changed by my life's experiences. I am not who I was 10 years ago, nor even who I was 5 years ago. And, 10 years from now, I doubt I will recognize the man who now writes this. The cycle of death and rebirth will forever be in my nature. I am no longer afraid of death.

People often say that this or that person has not yet found himself. But the self is not something one finds, it is something one creates.

Thomas Szasz, The Second Sin (1973)

Authors' Thoughts:

Tony says uttering the words, "I'm going to Switch Gears" sounds easy, but executing it is difficult. The fear of failure, if allowed, will always become an obstacle and make things difficult. Words that jump out when Tony talks about craftsmanship are PLEASURE, FASCINATION, CALMNESS, TRUE SATISFACTION and UNIQUE PRIDE. That is what we are all striving for in our lives. However, it appears that the fear of failure and being part of a convoluted world disappear when he's creating décor pieces for his club. Thus, Switching Gears becomes easier.

Reflections:

- What's the hardest things you've had to learn in your life that enabled you to Switch Gears?

- Do you have a paralyzing fear in your life? If so what is it and how did or do you overcome it?

- What are your hidden talents?

Teaching Point:

_____

What is my purpose? There are no rules!

7
BELIEVING IN YOURSELF

Your only limitations are those you set up in your mind,
or permit others to set up for you.

Og Mandino

Og Mandino's University of Success (1982)

Introduction:

This is a story of a friend who went through many trials and tribulations in pursuit of the ultimate career and to live in a place he loves and that reflects his values. This is nothing new for many of you who are reading and have not gone through it yourself, but what he learned about himself, we believe, may help those who haven't gotten to the place where BJ is today.

As for Switching Gears, the drawing could evoke an awakening – an awakening because you commit to Switching Gears only after realizing that change only comes through approaching things differently, charting a different path, climbing from fear that may have held you in place previously. You can spend your precious time in the box convincing yourself that things will change when you know in your heart they will not.

BJ's story:

For me, gaining comfort in Switching Gears was learned through life's practice; gaining experience at **trusting** myself and my decisions regardless of the outcome, and more importantly, learning from the risks taken.

My first recollection at having to Switch Gears came as a result of a failed marriage. I was presented with a start-up opportunity in the role of Vice President of Sales & Marketing for a high-tech semiconductor manufacturer. This opportunity came at a time when my marriage was already in shambles. Although I desperately wanted my marriage to succeed, I had to accept that this goal was mine alone and that I had to make the tough decision to seek divorce and gamble my future on change. That risk proved fruitful as the decision to *Switch Gears* afforded me many positive personal and financial outcomes that would never have been available if I had not chosen to take action.

After working for several years in start-up mode, we successfully sold our company to a well-known global manufacturer with whom I worked for years thereafter. Over time, when it became evident that my leadership opportunities were limited and the business was becoming stagnate, I was again faced with a key decision to *Switch Gears*. I chose to leave the company and form my own consulting business, trading the comfort of the W-2 relationship for that of a 1099 contractor. This risk also proved productive as I secured a role as VP of Sales & Marketing for a small company located in Arizona. The experience was quite rewarding as it forced me to **believe** in my capability to expand into an entrepreneurial role. However, that contract ended and I was out-of-work for almost 1½ years at a time when the stock market was poor and career options were scarce.

I eventually took an opportunity with a company located in Durham, NC. This new career came at a huge cost – relocation. I moved to Cary, NC and took a role managing sales in Europe, which was filled with many exciting challenges. Two years later, it became evident that I was being set-up for failure by this company and there was nothing I could do (as an outsider) to affect the outcome. Once again, it was time for me to **trust** in myself and use what I had learned from *Switching Gears* several times in the past. I needed to take control back from an unappreciative organization and route a new future for myself regardless of the outcome. Therefore, I decided that I would make my next decision based upon personal desires, not based upon necessity of having employment. Unbeknown to the firm, I purchased a home back in Charlotte, NC and began the plan of moving back to an area I enjoyed. Once the papers settled on the home purchase, I approached management and informed them of "changes". I communicated that I had purchased a home in Charlotte and that I would be moving effective immediately and suggested I could work from home to serve the clients affairs. This was unacceptable so the choice was to quit or be fired. I resigned and moved the following week back to Charlotte with no job, but to a new home and the comfort it provided as I took control of a bad situation and **trusted** my experiences.

Over the following year, I worked on my property and began looking for employment. One day, out of the blue, I discovered an exciting opportunity with a Swiss-based company that had relocated their domestic headquarters to Charlotte. Within one week, I was interviewed and had secured a new career. I have enjoyed every aspect of this new experience. And, more importantly, I have grown personally from all of my changes and risks into a person who has a greater awareness of what *Switching Gears* means in life and how important it is to **believe** in yourself and learn to **trust** in the outcome. Looking back, I have never regretted *Switching Gears*!

> *If you don't understand your limitations,*
> *you won't achieve much in your life.*

Kevin Costner, <u>Keeper of the Flame</u>
(March 15, 2001)

Authors' Thoughts:

What a testimonial this is for TRUSTING in yourself to reach your final outcome. As in the forward of our book, we discussed that there were key characteristics of people who were successful in Switching Gears. BJ reflects several of those in his story – trust, experience, a solid main gear and being clear on your purpose are essential. We have known BJ for over 18 years and as we read his story, it speaks to who he is even today as he lives in his beautiful home on Lake Norman. He has a 180 degree view of the lake and it's everything he envisioned when he began looking. He is still with the Swiss company that he uncovered in his job search, has been promoted from his original position and travels the world bringing value to the company every day.

Reflections:

_____

- Is going outside your comfort zone one of your strengths?

- Are you willing to leave a job or situation and with no idea of what you are going to do next?

- How trusting are you of yourself and others? Is this an obstacle for you Switching Gears?

- A key question throughout this book is "what is your purpose"? Have you defined it and does it guide your life?

Teaching Point:

Believe in yourself.

8
PUT ON YOUR HAPPY FACE

Introduction

This is a story of someone I've known almost 30 years and her story was totally unfamiliar to me. To know Charlotte today you would never imagine her life experiences. She is one of the most positive, funny, self-confident, smart and creative people I know and it is a pleasure to be involved with her both personally and professionally.

Charlotte's Story:

As far back as I can remember, I don't recall a time when I wasn't *Switching Gears*, or planning to do so. At the time, I didn't think of it that way, but that is exactly what it was. Even as a very young child, my memories were of having to avoid a situation that brought me pain, or perhaps better said, just didn't bring me any joy. My father, returning from WWII with what today would have been diagnosed as PTSD, turned to alcohol as a source of comfort by the time my memories were being formed – age 2 or 3. Years later, I can recall my parents friends', who had known him "before the war", telling me stories about a person I never knew. They described him as joyful, positive, good sense of humor, community-minded, a great dancer and dresser – an all-around great guy, they said. That was certainly not the guy who lived in our house – the one I called "daddy". And, while it sounds harsh, I can honestly say I felt no love for him – I don't recall having experienced a time where love could be learned.

My childhood memories were only of physical and verbal abuse, wet beds and furniture, hearing the slurring and inability to speak clearly or walk without falling and these images and experiences were not those that foster love or respect from a child. Today as I think back, I'm sure he was frustrated, lonely and sad, hurt, scared – what mental torture and awful memories he must have harbored. Those of us who have never been in war cannot comprehend a situation as awful as war must be, being shot at or seeing your buddy shot, or worse. There is no blame or resentment here towards my father; only disappointment and regret of having missed having him in my life. My mother, on the other hand, worked her entire life to support our family, a total of 5, without any emotional or financial support from my father. Oh, he held down a job – he was what we today call a "functioning alcoholic", but what he earned was spent on booze, clothes and cars. He was a well-dressed, flashy and charming drunk, always with the latest new automobile. I've often wondered if my mothers' constant criticism and inability to know or learn how to deal with the hand she had been dealt impacted his feelings of self-worth and self-esteem, further adding to his "pain". For the most part, I believe our parents do the best they know how to do so, again, there is no blame; just acceptance and understanding that was learned later in life. I know throughout those earliest years, I must have **Switched Gears** regularly to avoid depression because I don't harbor any memories of a "sad" or "unhappy" childhood; I don't have many memories at all. I remember no birthday parties, no friends, not even Christmas although I'm sure we celebrated because there are some pictures to prove it!

By the time I was 12, I had become a "parent" – another *Gear Switch*. I had to assume many of the responsibilities for my younger sister and brother, plus "seeing to" my dad. I was the one who helped them prepare for school, and the one who planned and prepared the meals, helped with homework in the afternoons, the laundry, the house cleaning, and the transportation of my siblings to get them to/from their game practices, piano lessons or whatever– it fell to me, the oldest, to pick up the slack. We simply didn't have the resources to hire help. By 13, I was driving my father's (flashy, new) car after school so that I could retrieve him from his favorite "watering hole". My mother owned her own business and worked more than 12 hours a day, generally from 7am to often well past 8pm, six days a week in order to pay the mortgage, utilities and buy clothes and groceries. It took that to support a family of 5. So, by the time I was 15, I was planning how to get the hell out! Unfortunately, it seemed then the only escape was marriage.

It turned out the young man I chose to marry simply wasn't a good choice, but I didn't know that at the time and, after all, he had been my high school sweetheart. Plus, without much foresight, it got me OUT – away from what I didn't think was "normal". Only a few months before our wedding, my future husband's dad, whom I had learned to love like a father, died suddenly of a heart attack. And, soon after we were married we discovered that the new mother-in-law, had been unfaithful to her husband for a number of years prior to his death, and had a sweetheart who had an attraction for young girls. Shortly after we were married, during a bad bout of the flu, he posed as a doctor and "examined" me – below the waist!!! – all with the full knowledge and support of my new mother-in-law. WOW – out of the frying pan into a real hot fire!

It wasn't too long after this event, that I made another plan – *Switch Gears*, leave yet another toxic relationship and, if nothing else, try it on your own! Oh, my mother offered me the use of my former bedroom in her house – NO WAY! I was already working full-time and going to college and while I knew the degree would take longer than the usual 4 years, a degree was the ticket to a better life. My mantra became – you can do ANYTHING for a short period of time – and it has served me well through many years. I bet I've said that to myself a thousand times or more. I remember at one of my jobs during college when my superior suggested we work on Saturdays, and "play footsies" – that's not what I meant by ANYTHING. I would rather be fired, and I promptly was! I did, however, repeat that to myself daily as part of my "self-talk" and still use it today during a difficult situation.

I managed to support myself by working 40-hour jobs and continuing to take classes that would eventually earn me that degree, although I will admit I struggled financially. One of our wedding gifts, from a grocery store owner, had been several cases of canned food – I remember eating Le Seuer Peas for so long that, even today, I gag at the mere thought of them! The bed in my efficiency apartment was a recliner – after all, it served more than one purpose! There were times I couldn't afford to take the next class I needed, but I continued to work and skimp and save literally every single penny I could. I most often took jobs that would allow me to continue school which often meant I worked strange hours.

I may have been an early pioneer for the concept "working from home" – as long as the work was completed, there didn't seem to be a problem where I was physically located. At one place, an older gentleman, some 18 years my senior, took me under his wing and encouraged me in every way possible to stay on my path. When I would appear to be discouraged, I still recall his frequent reminders that it wasn't the end of the world if it took "forever" to get that degree as long as you got it! That sort of support and concern soon lead to admiration, which turned to love, and eventually we were married. He had received his undergraduate degree from the University of South Carolina (Go Gamecocks!) and did his graduate work at the University of Georgia so football games and all the parties that come with that crowd were a big part of our "fun". He owned his own plane and even later taught me to fly. He was so smart; witty, a great dancer and community-minded, and a good dresser – sound like someone else?! Yep, I had fallen in love with and married my father! And for 12 years, we were relatively happy – owned a "ranch", had horses and had great parties! Alcohol was a big part of our life and, over time it became apparent that when he drank, he drank too much and could become abusive, both physically and verbally – another trait of my father! But, because he was a trained therapist, we didn't seek help and so we continued our life until there was nothing left but lost souls.

It seemed I had a penchant of making bad decisions in my personal life. Reminds me of a song by Conway Twitty - "Looking for Love in All the Wrong Places". So, once again, I made a plan to *Switch Gears.*

Actually, truth be told, this time my plan for *Switching Gears* included NEVER marrying again. I did just fine by myself, had reached the point where, financially, I was comfortable so why risk it?! For a few years, that thought prevailed, but then, once again, I met someone and through friendship, we fell in love and married. I guess I wanted to be half of a couple – that felt normal to me.

However, that marriage ended after 21 years – quite suddenly and to my complete shock and deep sadness, and it involved a younger woman – you've heard that story before! And, for me, it was the first time I *Switched Gears* without a plan. I had been caught off guard – in a flash, during lunch on a Friday, I had lost my husband, my friend, my love, my job (we had been co-owners in a business) and because we lived in a small, resort town which had less than 10,000 "residents", I knew I also had to include a physical relocation in my plan – I knew I could not bear running into "them", which was highly probable. This meant selling my home, moving to another city and moving away from some very close friends – starting over with everything! In hindsight, it turned out to be a blessing because it gave me the opportunity to create my future, in whatever city I chose, and no longer be dependent upon anyone else to meet my emotional needs. I had been okay on my own previously, I could do that again. I had amassed two handfuls of great, long-time, dear friends, was able to travel and enjoy parts of the world that interested me with whomever I chose to be with. Life became and still is good.

Today, I am now almost "fully" retired (I still "dabble" at some projects) after having had a rewarding career. I loved what I did, made many friends and still keep in touch with a number of people I met and mentored throughout those working years; some were clients, some were employees and some just friends from as far back as my college days. I worked full-time until I was 70, and while I was employed mostly by family-owned businesses during my career, I did own two companies myself. I continue to mentor young people who have chosen my same industry. My most cherished volunteer work is whatever I can offer to the residents of "A Room at the Inn", a place for unwed pregnant girls, sponsored at and by a local university. I often share my choices with them in an effort to guide them in making better decisions for themselves. I also teach computer and software program skills so they will be prepared to start over after their baby is born and adopted. While I am usually only in their life for a few months, some good friendships have grown from my work. It helps them when I share some of the wisdoms learned from my life and mistakes. I try to bestow lessons that will help them:

1.   Don't wallow in your sorrows or misfortunes – there are always people less fortunate than you and

it is not positive behavior – no one really wants to be around it.

2. Smile – always - it could be the only positive thing in someone's entire day. Put your best face forward.

3. Find a solution to your mistakes – a good solution. Sometimes it's too close to recognize.

4. When you're having a bad day, know that tomorrow will be better. If it's not, then the day after that will be!

5. Try to learn something new every day that will benefit you tomorrow. You can never have too much knowledge.

Retirement – yet another *Gear Switch* – can be one of the best seasons in your life – it provides a freedom unlike anything that can be imagined. It can also be a time for reflection with the opportunity to understand things that happened to you during your life and while you can't change them nor should you wish them "undone", you learn to embrace them as teaching experiences and share that knowledge of learning and understanding with those younger who are passing through their lives undecided about their specific *Gear* Switch. I love to read, knit and do needlepoint, and enjoy visiting the coast of NC where my gracious niece maintains "my room" at her second home beside the ocean. You can bet I'm there as often as possible! Today I have a wonderful, trustful, honest and caring gentleman in my life who was once one of that collection of friends. We met in 1980, *Switched Gears* in 1996 to "other than friends", and were married in 2016 – 20 years after the *Switch,* but I was determined to be absolutely CERTAIN this time! We were once good friends, and now we are a great couple as we enjoy each other's company, share the same humor (which is very important!) love and cherish each other and provide support and encouragement to one another every day.

Author's Thoughts:

As we read Charlotte's story, what came to mind isn't something we've not seen or heard before, the significant difference was that Charlotte kept consciously *Switching Gears*, looking for a better life.

Reflections:

- As you read Charlotte's story, what attributes did you see in her? Are those attributes you have or aspire to have?

- Was there a theme to her story? If so, what was it?

- What do you believe is Charlotte's greatest learning about Switching Gears?

Teaching Point:

_____

Learning to be a survivor rather than a victim is critical to successfully *Switching Gears.*

9
ROSE COLORED GLASSES

Introduction:

This is a story of an awesome lady who, in addition to being tenacious and compassionate, loves unconditionally, cares beyond comprehension, and is smart and willing to learn. She is also the love of my life! Prior to Switching Gears following my cancer diagnosis, Bonnie was a care giver as she raised 4 daughters, and she continues to give care when she occasionally babysits her grandkids. She has a long-held distrust of the medical system and doctors in general, which came about when her father passed away after having been prescribed the wrong medication. The only medicine she takes today is gummy bears. She doesn't routinely go to doctors nor does she have the typical annual exam. Her belief system is "it will get better, whatever it is". As a matter of fact, she lanced a growth on her own ear (that should have been seen by a dermatologist) – it healed fortunately. Quick funny story - she is frequently harassed by her family about getting a colonoscopy and after finally acquiescing and setting an appointment, COVID-19 came along and the facility called to cancel it! Missed the bullet again!

Bonnie's Story:

My world changed forever overnight when Terry was diagnosed with Multiple Myeloma in January of 2017 and required me to quickly *Switch Gears.* I was totally out of my element, didn't know who to call or how to navigate the medical world starting with calling health care clinics, hospitals, primary care physicians and numerous other potential providers. Every one told me it would be 3 to 9 months before we could be seen. We simply just did not have that time as he already had lesions all over his body and was in severe pain. I was in a panic, not knowing where to turn nor who to call until, finally, venting to my daughter, Ashley, she gave me the name of a personal friend who was also the COO of Lennar Medical Center in Coral Gables, and suggested I contact him. One call to Ben and he took control. The next thing I know is that we had appointments set up with the people who could and did help us.

So began my new role of care giver and patient advocate with doctors, nurses, interpreter of orders, meds and procedures. I became Terry's eyes and ears for everything that concerned him. I liked both doctors right away because they engaged me as well as our families but, most of all, they engaged Terry in every aspect of his treatment and care. I was very impressed when both doctors openly let our daughters, Jenny and Heather, into the consultations about the condition and procedures ahead. They patiently answered all our questions and especially the ones from Jenny because she is in the medical field and hers were ones that would never have occurred to the rest of us. When they couldn't answer the questions, they said they would get back to her, AND THEY DID! That enamored me to them which made it considerably easier to transition into my role as care giver. Initially, we spent 16 days in the hospital trying to get the pain under control while at the same time beginning treatment. The doctors had placed a rod into Terry's femur from the knee to his hip rendering him completely immobile for some time. That required extra care giver tasks for a rookie.

I practically lived at the hospital. I was there every day, all day and, during this period, I even spent the nights to be available to Terry at any moment. During the afternoon, I would often return home to shower and nap since sleeping at the hospital didn't give me much rest. There were many times Terry had to console me as

I cried my eyes out on the way to and from the hospital, literally scared to death. I got some relief when Heather came to stay with her Dad in the hospital and then Jenny came when we finally were able to go home.

I protected Terry from visitors and screened his phone calls. Heather set up and then taught me how to use Group Facebook® so I could send out weekly updates rather than having to singularly manage information to our friends and family. I also learned about medications, MRI's, CAT scans, diabetes management, and how to move Terry, and I learned to watch Terry's eyes and know when the pain hit 15 and when it subsided. Together we celebrated small successes, like the first time getting out of bed and going to the bathroom by himself! I also had to demonstrate tough love with him, focusing on him getting better and going home. I endured his steroid nights when he was so wired, creating, writing, talking non-stop, and singing all night long. Neither one of us got much sleep during those days. When the decision came whether to go to a rehab center or go home, I was the one who urged the decision to go home and do rehab there.

Unbeknownst to all, I was preparing our home for both his arrival and his rehab. Gabby, our dog, who was still with us then and had been staying with Ashley's family, would become instrumental to keeping Terry's mental health upbeat. Not having to go back and forth to the hospital every day was a great relief for me and allowed my entire focus to be on Terry and his needs. Not having to leave home, get in and out of the car, and into and out of a rehab facility made things somewhat easier. *Switching* **Gears** to a full-time care giver was a challenge for me but one I accepted with love.

I remember the day we were to check Terry out of the hospital; I was being bombarded by a Walgreens representative who was explaining all the drugs we were to take home and the schedules for each: OxyContin, Hydrocortisone, Metformin, Acyclovir, Fentanyl patches, steroids – so many that I felt completely overwhelmed. Terry had to take control to get rid of the representative for me. We finally got the hospital concierge, Adrienne, to help us by getting a wheelchair to get him out of the room and eventually out of the hospital. Oh my God, helping us get Terry into the car and then us driving down the ramp away from University of Miami hospital was very emotional for both of us. Crying, but at the same time embracing every sight and sound as if it were the first time.

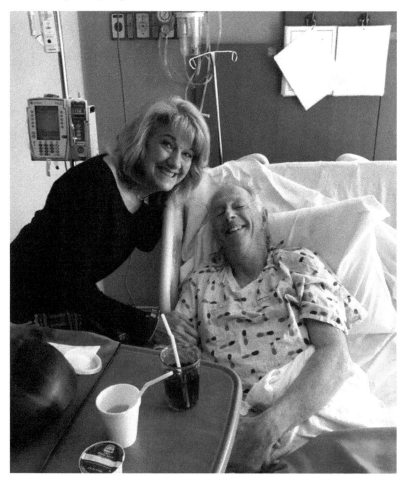

The next chapter of my **G***ear* **S***witch* was about to begin from how things had become somewhat normal to now we were going to be doing them on our own at home. New shower chair, new shower railings, canes from Italy as well as the University of Florida (see pictures), a heightened toilet seat and a walker – all waiting for Terry. The first thing he did was to sit down in the shower for 30 minutes and drown himself with a hot shower. I had to help him step down the 3" into the shower and also a 3" drop onto our outside patio. And there was Gabby by Terry's side every step of the way. She was such an awesome care dog!

Gabby

Our neighbors came to help in every and any way they could; bringing us food, offering to run errands or to stay with Terry, allowing me to get away. I remained his protector, deciding who to allow in or not allow in when visitors dropped by, and I continued to screen his phone calls so as not to tire him out. I updated everyone each week regarding his condition, drove him to the clinics for treatments and met with Drs. Hoffman and Al Maaieh. I organized all of his meds and kept him on schedule.

I need to say here that I was a woman totally unfamiliar with the medical system, and was also very distrusting. My versatility changed to an amiable driver. My total focus was on Terry so that he would be able to walk again and eventually obtain some kind of new normalcy in our lives. I remember when we got home in Weston, I had bought Terry an art kit. And because he initially had no interest, I was disappointed as I had tried so hard to have things for him to do to occupy his time. But, I realized he just wasn't ready for it, but then, one day he picked it up and began painting.

I was eventually able to get out and play some golf, or canasta with my friends just to get a break from care giving. I would visit my mom, sister and brother only if I knew Terry would be OK. Gradually, I **Switched Gears** to one of maintaining a routine for both of us. The staff at the hospital was great, and Terry journaled about the really good people there like Tarquizza, Juan, Michael, Dr. Levy and others. My role today is prescription organizer, morale supporter and listener. I established my own doctors at Sylvester - Caroline Rinehart, a primary care physician and an eye doctor. And I fell in love with our concierge, Cynthia, and we became good friends, especially when she had her first grandchild.

Sometimes *Switching Gears* is thrust upon us and the skills we learned early in life come into play. In order to be effective, we must learn to deal with ambiguity, become comfortable being uncomfortable, and challenge prior belief systems. This is how I learned to Switch Gears without knowing how!

Authors' Thoughts:

I don't think we can add anymore to Bonnie's final paragraph – it sums up our thoughts exactly.

Reflections:

When I think back on that journey, and it continues today, our relationship has grown closer than ever. There are times when my emotions are not very versatile but Bonnie's are. She continues to learn to have patience with the patient.

- What belief or beliefs do you have that may be hindering your ability to *Switch Gears*?

- What life experiences do you have that could help you excel at *Switching Gears*?

- How comfortable are you being uncomfortable and dealing with ambiguity? What is an example?

Teaching Point:

One must learn to be "comfortable in an uncomfortable" situation. Understand behavioral styles especially when stress is prevalent in a situation. Take care of yourself; so important.

10
HAVING NO CONTROL,
BUT THERE IS A WAY

Satu

Introduction

About the time we were getting close to finishing this book, COVID-19 hit and the pandemic set in across the world. We thought if there ever was an event that would require everyone to Switch **G**ears, this was it! We knew our lives were forever changed and *Switching* **G***ears* is the competency we must learn.

Our Story:

At one time, many of the events that we will discuss in this book would have been considered the most devastating happening in the life of a business or an individual. However, that was before the COVID-19 Pandemic rocked everyone's world across the globe. Businesses were hit with massive unemployment, many had to furlough or lay-off staff; some had to close their doors, all mandated by either the government or scientific community in an effort to stop the spread of the virus. It required every one of us to S*witch* **G**ears. What we did every day and how we did it was no longer the same. Eating at a restaurant, getting a haircut or manicure, attending an event whether indoors or outdoors, attending church, even visiting the dentist or doctor all changed. Elective surgery was postponed so that hospital beds and medical services were reserved for those with the virus. Large gatherings such as football games, NASCAR races, and PGA tournaments were all suddenly halted because of the interaction with other humans along with the risk of contracting and/or spreading the virus.

Everyone was in lockdown – they were told to stay "in place" – most of us in our homes – and only venture out for essential items such as food, medicine, etc. A major **Gear S**witch – on-line shopping hit an all-time high, groceries were either retrieved outside the grocery store or were delivered to our homes – alcohol, prescriptions and food – all delivered. Schools went virtual; visiting friends or family face-to-face stopped; all socializing was halted. "Social distancing" became a new, often heard term. Nothing was normal as we had known it. Uncertainty surrounded everything. Zoom® became the way to hold meetings, attend concerts or talk with family and friends. People who had worked all their lives stood in lines to draw unemployment while many learned they could earn more through this program than when they actually worked for a paycheck. Unemployment got close to the 30 percentile in America! Most everyone wore masks when venturing outside their home, either to help prevent spreading the virus or in an attempt to prevent contracting it. Fear gripped our nation because this virus was unpredictable and deadly, but even worse, *it was invisible*! There was no experience with it, and in the beginning, no one was even certain how it was transmitted. The elderly in nursing homes were isolated, often seeing family only through windows. Initially this was the source of unprecedented spread due to the confinement of the facility itself. Too often we would hear stories of someone dying without having any family member present and only having contact through a cellphone being held by medical staff. OUT OF CONTROL – that's what it felt like, and it was! Everyday there was new thinking around **S**witching **G**ears in every aspect of our lives. We had to redefine "normal", create ways to do business differently and look for alternative ways to generate income.

And then along came another unplanned event which touched the lives of so many. Protests and riots broke out as a result of the death of a black man who was being restrained by white police officers. People were angry; stores were looted, people were killed or injured in many of the major cities in the US. Just as everyone was beginning to reopen restaurants and small businesses, this disturbance was devastating to everyone who were already in crisis mode. So *Switching* **Gears** again, and not knowing just what to do. Never before have our families, homes, cities, country – our WORLD – been faced with such a catastrophe. People felt as if, just when they were beginning to adjust or recover, **BAM** – another punch in the gut.

In order to survive and thrive, it required all of us to *Switch* **Gears**. And it is certain we will continue in this state until a vaccine is discovered – perhaps 18 months or longer.

Authors' Reflections on the PANDEMIC

First visuals of the PANDEMIC

The word "PANDEMIC" strikes fear in the hearts and minds of people. In response to the deadly COVID-19, Canadian Prime Minister Justin Trudeau exclaimed, "It's time for all Canadians abroad to come home". Unbeknownst to me, my wife, Marlene, had already packed me up two weeks before the call to return home. She knew that I would be in no rush to leave beautiful, warm, sunny Florida. We had to leave a week before the birthday celebration of Jordyn, our granddaughter who lives in Florida, to "get out of Dodge", and to quickly escape to a land that seemed safer with far fewer cases. We packed our cooler full of peanut butter and jam sandwiches, nuts, fruits, veggies and loads of water and juice. We couldn't fathom stopping at a restaurant to eat, imagining the food having been touched or breathed upon by someone potentially with this deadly virus. Everything was wrapped in fear. We had 23 hours of road ahead of us and our mantra as we kept driving was, "Be Mindful, Be Mindful!!!" At a gas station, we used a disposable wipe to hold the handle of the gas pump and, after having inserted our credit card in the slot to pay, we wiped it clean with another wipe. REMEMBER – Do not touch your beard or face! Sit on your hands if you have to! Always have a mask, sanitizer and wipes within reach.

As we were driving home through the mountains and it began growing dark, we started searching for a town and a place to spend the night. At the hotel we chose, only a few of the staff were working, which was a very strange feeling. How can they possibly sanitize the rooms? Dare I shower or take a bath? Although breakfast was included with the room, dare I take a banana?

Marlene was anxious and in a real hurry to get home. The only delay was the one day a speeding ticket was issued to guess who? I had texted this message to Terry: "Marlene rarely gets a ticket when she's driving but guess what??? The officer, trying to be helpful, suggested she might want to come back and fight it – YEAH RIGHT!" Terry interjected his thought, "Do you even want to take it from him? To touch it?"

One can only go for so long without having to use the restroom, so eventually we pulled into a rest area. Our anxiety level shot up as we tried to imagine how we were going to open the door to the restroom without bumping into someone on the other side. What if we had to wait in line for the next stall – would someone get too close? Are the stalls being cleaned between each use? Once inside the stall, how do we lower our garments without them touching or making contact with something? How do we gradually sit down on the toilet seat without touching anything or would we lose our balance? Are our abs strong enough to allow us to perch above the seat without touching it?

The irony of the world today reminded me of two movies from my childhood. The first one was "War of the Worlds", where alien beings, half alive and half dead, were invading our bodies and were eventually destroyed because THEY were not immune to a bacteria in our atmosphere. Aliens – killed by a virus! Who would have thought? The other movie was from 1951, in black and white and was titled "The Day the Earth Stood Still". I was 9 years old at the time I saw it and it had a profound impact on me. The "alien" had a mission to exterminate the human race. It is still considered a classic today of the genre that reflects the fears and anxieties of the peoples on the earth. How closely similar that is to what we have all experienced in the year of 2020. The question arises, interestingly, is it possible that there is opportunity coming from this event – perhaps there is a doorway from the past to the future?

This pandemic has impacted every aspect of all of our lives. We have new rules we must learn; simple but imperative, beginning with something as simple as "DON'T TOUCH YOUR FACE". We must be extremely mindful not to shake anyone's hand – bumping elbows or fists is the new "greeting". We say "COVID-19" easily and are learning to redefine "NORMAL". That, in and of itself, has created tremendous anxiety. There are travel bans worldwide; the stock market plunged. There is tremendous uncertainty, which leads to anxiety. Survival is determining what's safe and what's not.

We now are changing our definitions of **TRUST, FEAR, UNCERTAINTY,** and **POSITIVES that create OPPORTUNITY.**

UNCERTAINTY

How do you *Switch Gears* when you can't plan or prepare yourself? We construct illusions of certainty, convincing ourselves that we can count on the arrival of tomorrow, next year and 10 or more years from now. We pretend we can plan; then along comes COVID-19 and our plans are turned upside down and backwards in an instant. We live in a deluded, defended world where we often fool ourselves that we can predict the future, so when we *Switch Gears,* we know where we're going.

Uncertainty is a common fact of daily living; it is everywhere and ever-present, yet we prefer to avoid it or deny it whenever possible. With COVID-19, our defenses are more challenged and have been tested like never before; thus, we have to accept the extraordinary uncertainty more. We just can't deny it like we used to. It is important that we don't put a value judgement on which uncertainty is more worthy whether it's tragic, sad or challenging. The garden variety of uncertainty is just as important – don't get caught up in whether one is more legitimate than another. Millions of people are burdened by their uncertainties – one has a shattered leg and the other a hangnail – it doesn't mean the hangnail doesn't hurt. Avoid this thinking; it's not about who has it worse.

We must be mindful that not everyone views this time of uncertainty in the ways described above. They are scared to death of what each moment, day or week might bring. Many have lost their jobs, or had to close a business; lost their home or are not being able to put food on the table for their family. Helping people to view places of uncertainty as places of great opportunity is our purpose.

First comes acknowledgement of their current reality and to stay present with it even when it's challenging. We must face the grief or fear and stay focused on a positive outcome. The emotions and thoughts will be like a roller coaster, which is normal. In addition, we must learn to recover from change through remaining self-aware; we must be mindful and encourage positive relationships. As a result, one can develop skills such as activating positive emotions and cultivating a belief in your ability to cope and help others.

POSITIVES CREATING OPPORTUNITY

The quarantine has presented a number of opportunities even though many saw it as a great inconvenience. It gave us time to reflect, plus time to purge or, perhaps, for me, time to pursue another interest. It provided us the time to connect with friends and family like never before. A particular experience for me was to look up a relative with whom I had lost touch over the years, but of whom I was especially fond. I was reminded of him as I recalled a book by Holling C. Holling, "Paddle-To-The-Sea", which is one of my favorite children's books and is an adventure of epic proportions, awakening a longing for nature and adventure. It fired my imagination and inspired my love of nature. As a new beginning, and being in a location where I was in touch with nature caused me to think of a loved one who was struggling at this time, so I sent my nephew in the UK the following note:

"Hi Jake! I was thinking about you today as I was paddling my canoe. I feel invigorated with the wind and breeze against my face and challenged by the rolling whitecaps. The sun is glistening off the water. With each stroke of the blade, I enter a euphoric state of peace. Whipping up the waves, the force of the wind knocks my bow off course. My arms feel like they're going to fall off as I muscle the elements. I'm in battle mode, to conquer or be conquered. I now stand in front of the mirror, my upper body transformed from loose and flabby to rock solid. Physically, I feel so much stronger, and mentally I feel so much sharper. Daily, for 6 plus weeks, dedicated and committed, I embrace the day, full of hope and a renewed sense of purpose. This every day ritual has helped lift my

*spirits, clear my head and recharge my batteries as I
search for new beginnings.*

Love you very much. Joel

With a virgin, unspoiled canvas, I wave my hands like a
maestro; in place of a baton, I roll the paintbrush between my
fingers and sway to the music; I swoop down and let my body and
the brush lead the way. I'm lost in the moment, unaware of any
existence around me. The beginning of creation. I'm discovering
everything for the first time. I'm challenging the canvas to give it
life. Let it go, let it go! I turn my head off and just fly with it. I try
dancing with my hands in time to my voice bellowing ♫ ♫ tra..
la..la.la..la ♫ ♫ freeing me up and firing my creative juices, all the
while releasing the child within me. At times, I close my eyes and
feel the line with my body. Then, I open my eyes and whatever
associations come to me, I venture forth, the final product is a
surprise to me! Again, "There are no rules."

As strange as it may sound, here are some other positives
that were a result of COVID-19:

- Working from home has been quite a surprise to
  both the employee and the employer. From the
  employees standpoint, it has given them great
  flexibility; no wasted time commuting, often less
  interruptions unless there is home schooling.
  Plus, there is the savings of wardrobe expenses.
  A downside, however, is that many employees are
  finding they work longer hours each day while
  actually being more productive. This works as
  a plus for employers, who are learning they are
  having to give up control; not knowing what each

employee is doing each day and having to trust that they are performing. Many companies have never favored a work from home at-home policy and are now finding that they must find new ways to measure the staff. What that really means is that now they have to actually measure performance, not face time in the office. We think that working from home, whatever that is, is a new reality and may become a new normal as employers begin to learn the advantages and cost savings of reducing rent reduction, utilities, etc. that can impact the bottom line.

- On-line learning and/or home schooling has both positive and negative effects. Obviously, the students are missing the contact with their peers that can impact social skills. Many students felt that connection was the best of the school day. As sad as it is, we have found that some students do not have internet access while others are unable to access the apps that are required. Also, there may not be space in the home for a designated area to learn, and there could be unexpected interruptions from parents or siblings. The positive aspects, however, can include flexibility, not having to hurry to catch buses, and a reduction to the exposure to the virus. It could possibly accelerate their learning as it allows for more focus. This could quite likely be the way education will move forward in the future. It will mean less brick and mortar for colleges. It will also affect professors, administrators and challenge the staff as the need to support the students' changes.

- Grocery shopping has become less of a hassle with delivery, drive-up loading at the store from on-line shopping. The convenience of this task is most attractive and has already set another "new normal" routine for many. Some miss the actual shopping experience that allows for roaming the stores and finding new products, but most people are really enjoying this new service. We think we will probably see new businesses created that will add more value with this service and potentially established businesses adding "mobile shopping" as one of its services.

- Outside dining is becoming a savior for many of the restaurants that are trying to survive COVID-19. We've seen a number of instances where there is cooperation between the restaurant(s) and the city or town to close off a street that was once open to vehicles and using that space for dining during certain hours. One of the challenges they may face is related to the weather when the accommodations can't provide a covered area. This could be very helpful to the restaurant business, especially as long as the occupancy is limited. Plus, many people do not feel safe inside a building where air circulation may be a contributor for spreading the virus.

- Many have found pursuing passions (art, music, writing, new business venture) to be challenging. But, for others, this time provided an opportunity to pursue interests that were previously dormant. For us, we both have pursued art and also completed this book.

- Large dinners with family and friends are a thing of the past until we find a vaccine for this virus. Now we have dinners and celebrations via Zoom™ and they have become a treasured part of the day/week/season. It provides time to catch up with each other, stay in touch with school, help with issues and emotions some may be experiencing as well as just seeing the faces of loved ones. We are doing "drive by" celebrations, handing gifts through car windows. As a member of the "older generation", we find we still yearn for hugs from our children, grandchildren and friends.

- For those who could afford it, the pandemic gave us time for reflection. A time, perhaps, to look at our lives, create new purpose and value. A time to reflect where we are in our lives and what we may want to change or improve upon. One instance that is particularly poignant was Joel's conversation with a cousin with whom he had lost contact with for over 20 years. One day, shaking, teary-eyed, entrapped with emotion, after just spoken to him by phone….."Hi. It's Joel Walker speaking. I've been thinking about you and wanted to know that you were safe and self-isolating. I care about you. I know we haven't communicated in a long time but you were very important to me in the past and I wanted you to know that I was thinking of you and hoping you are well."

- Home Projects are becoming a big positive as people are spending more time in their homes. Renovating, adding pools, recreation rooms, outdoor areas with fire pits, barbecue grills and lounging areas. The other phenomenon we are seeing is people relocating their residences to the mountains, beaches or other more remote areas away from the crowded cities or moving to their second homes to live permanently. This is causing real estate values to increase and to sell quickly, sometimes sight unseen.

- Recreational vehicle sales exploded because people can travel and feel safe while they see the country. Very limited international travel will fuel this change.

There are many more positives that have come as a result of the pandemic and more are being created as we continue to adjust to the situation.

SILENCE

Quieting and calming the mind creates a heightened awareness because your mind is freed from the endless cycle of thinking, which can be distracting. When you silence your mind, your ability to focus improves, you can think more clearly, your comprehension increases and your awareness of the world around you expands. Being in self-isolation as a result of COVID has offered us that silence; some have embraced it while others found that *Gear Switch* as yet another challenge as interacting with people was the part of their day they most enjoyed.

FEAR

Nature feeds my soul; I feel one with nature as the trees whisper to me. Waving their arms, they beckon me. I feel calm and at peace. Lost and found, I'm lost in nature and at the same time, I'm found, like finding myself. At the end of the road, at the end of the lake, there is no one in sight. I breathe in, savoring the earthy scents and evocative odors of early spring. I feel so alive. I have no fear. I'm not bored for a moment. Enveloped in a canopy of green, all I see are trees, lake, sky and the far unknown. For 10 weeks, I've been immersed in natures lap. Time out of time – I'm trying to be open to what's happening, putting my intentions out there without pushing anything. Witnessing the awaking of this time of year, I treasure this rare opportunity.

Then, the first time we came out of self-isolation, having been nestled with nature and peace for almost 4 months, to take a dreaded trip to Toronto (in July of 2020) was an experience in fear. We were fearful of where to stop along the way or where to eat – all due to the pandemic. There were speed limits along the way, of course, but it seemed many were not heeding them. There were oodles of cars crowding the roads, many of those inhabitants fearful like us. The traffic was often "stop and go" and it was bloody hot in the car! There were 4 wheeled monsters rolling along with red tail lights flashing. Signs for wild strawberries, canoe outlets and gas stations, all intruding into my green world of nature. The beauty of the landscape was interrupted by an ugly, grey, asphalt highway. My view was muddied by the scattering of box stores and silos. We felt crowded between a guardrail and trailered vehicles with their watercraft, sleepy SUV's and gaudy colored compacts. Unnerving music blasted in my ears from the cars passing by – there was no escape from the rude awakening of quiet, shattering the fabric of my soul. HELP! A return to sanity, I cry for stillness, for solitude, for silence. Yikes! I'm in a concrete and steel jungle.

Now that I'm home, I feel less bombarded. The trip was because I was to have my bi-yearly MRI screening at North York General Hospital in Toronto. I had been procrastinating with trepidation, fearful of the presence of COVID-19, knowing that it existed in the very place I was headed – THE HOSPITAL! I kept putting it off, even reluctant to set up an appointment; rationalizing, and wondering how to weigh the odds. Then I kept seeking reassurance from my neurologist that it would be clean, sanitized and safe. I didn't want to be foolish and miss a potentially treatable situation by not going, but I didn't want COVID-19 either! Several months passed by and finally the time came when I just had to bite the bullet. So I ventured forth armed with gloves, masks and wipes. I had dressed in very loose clothing so I could quickly disrobe and so as to not remain in the changing room one second longer than necessary. I had phoned the MRI department a number of times in advance of even going to the hospital to make sure I had a detailed floor plan so as not to lose my way or be there any longer than absolutely necessary! I wanted to be prepared for all eventualities. Then, rumbling and roaring, the machine took all of its pictures as I lay completely still for 25 minutes with my eyes closed. Then, I quickly changed back into my street clothes and, with my mask still on, exited the hospital and took a deep breath!

TRUST

Perhaps not only as a result of the pandemic, but also perhaps due to the political climate today including the many social issues and injustices we perceive, many of us are questioning trust – who we trust, what we trust, when we trust and even why we trust, or don't. Many no longer trust the news, or printed material. We are required to research what we hear in order to form our opinions. Many are asking, "What can we believe?" It's a time so different than ever before and COVID-19 has added to the lack of trust. Was/is it real? Was/is it avoidable? Was/is it as bad as reported? Or is it over-hyped for health reporting and funding purposes?

Through my tone of voice, energy level and non-threatening behavior, I engaged my new, normally jumpy, bushy-tailed friend, without bribery of food, to form a trusting relationship. The red squirrel is a very skittish, feisty and spirited rodent. I have spent more hours chatting with my new four-legged friends than ever before. In an engaging, high pitched, friendly and upbeat voice, I often begin with, "Hi! Hey Bud, what's up? What ya doing?" OR "Hi, my name is Joel! What's yours?" My words just keep tumbling out; I have no idea what I'm going to say next, I just fly by the seat of my pants. It's like talking to my little grandkids. Dr. Doolittle – "They see me as one of them. Their answers are squirrelly." It's nice to know you're learning to communicate!

11
LESSONS FROM COVID-19

As we worked through this book, we wanted to include some real life experiences of the pandemic and its effect on members of the population in hopes to be a part of a plan for the future. We asked for feedback and posed specific questions to several people. Here are some of the responses:

Heather Todd
Director of Systems
National Home Services Franchisor

Q: In thinking of these last 90 or so days, tell us what you consider to be the most significant Gear Switch?

A: Managing my daughter with virtual school and myself with a booming business changing by the day. We have completely revamped the way we sell franchises, train new owners, and support existing ones all in a virtual world.

Q: What surprised you the most?

A: The fact that no one has missed a beat! Our company transitioned everyone home and switched an in-person training to virtual two days before it was to happen. That was March of this year and now our entire company has moved the majority of positions virtual permanently. We have continued to thrive and our workforce is happier. This from a company who use to say "All roads lead to Texas"!

Q: What skills or experiences helped you navigate through the quarantine?

A: Questioning skills, one of our core values is "Asking clarifying questions". The best way to identify a challenge, uncover a goal, celebrate a success, determine a new solution, and many more key areas is to ask questions! Questions help you learn someone's why and what they value.

Q: What lessons did you learn?

A: When you understand more you can transform what you provide in real time. You can *Switch Gears* while in motion.

Q: What new talents, creations or opportunities did you discover while dealing with the pandemic?

A: Reminded to prioritize who and what are important in your life. Continue to grow and learn while supporting those who might be stuck. Great growth and great opportunity will come out of great challenges.

Q: In what way did you Switch Gears?

A: Our family changed in our daily activities and reminded ourselves to focus back on the key things in life- relationships, love, laughter, caring, and fun! We all have been impacted by the pandemic, thankfully we have not been impacted extremely financially which has reminded us to always be thankful.

Q: What wisdom can you share about either your personal experience of Switching Gears or that of a friend or peer from whom you drew strength?

A: The COO of our organization shared a leadership strategy with our teams. During the height of the COVID-19 lock down our franchise owners were scared and there was so much uncertainty. We were navigating changes by the day and often by the hour. Mary Thompson shared that as leaders we do not have to know all the answers but we need to help our community move forward by "whistling in the dark". Continue to communicate and say "walk this way", "take this next step", "we are all in this together" and eventually we would get to the light. It was a game changer for our organization and our franchise owners!

Q: What will you change in your life in anticipation of either a resurgence of this virus or possibly another unforeseen crisis?

A: Plan more, prepare more, and be more purposeful in living. Life is a gift that sometimes we take for granted.

Angela McCoy
Chief Operations Officer
MyEyeDr

Q: In thinking of these last 90 or so days, tell us what you consider to be the most significant Gear Switch?

A: Our leadership team transitioned from strategic initiatives to day to day business management. Suddenly, like a light switch, we had decisions to make based on furlough, health benefits and general employee safety that affected the business in immediate ways. We quickly took inventory of business projects currently in flight and realigned our teams to be able to focus on day by day decisions.

Q: What surprised you the most? What skills or experiences helped you navigate through the lockdown?

A: Each day felt like a week, each week felt like a month. Work life balance was simply work. As the days went on, it became important to recognize the goals of each phase, celebrate the accomplishments and move to the next phase. For example reopening offices after being closed required a team, establishing the group of offices, protocols, plans, assessments, review, improvements to then move to the next phase. Once we were past reopening came the staffing phase, rebalancing the needs of the office with new safety and cleaning protocols. We leveraged associates with a growth mindset, those team members that were willing to do whatever it took to reopen. We leaned on technology, specifically Microsoft teams to have video calls and project management systems to keep each project visible and aligned throughout the organization. We created new reports to give us quick views on what was working.

Q: What lessons did you learn?

A: To take breaks. Self-Care is important and doesn't get enough publicity. You can't take care of associates if you don't take care of the business. You can't take care of the business if you don't take care of you. During the pandemic, everyone is going through lots of things, emotions, personal decisions, fear of the unknown. Everyone processes in a different way and pace. We have to be considerate of ourselves and each other.

Q: What new talents, creations or opportunities did you discover while dealing with the pandemic?

A: People will rise to the occasion if given the opportunity and training. Clearly communicate. Plan, Write out speeches, practice, and then record them on a video. Communicate often. In this day, team members can get news anytime, in whatever mode they want. Organizations need to communicate all of the time. Delegation shows people you trust them.

Q: In what way did you Switch Gears?

A: I assumed the role of COO in January, roughly 90 days before closing our offices for COVID-19, then reopening them 45 days later after we had obtained the PPE needed to operate safely. I learned you can't predict actions. You have to be ready for anything. To be ready for anything you have to prepare for anything, to practice. That preparation got me through long days. Know how your day is going to go before it happens. Know what 3 things you have to get out of a meeting. Be more intentional with time and activity to ensure success.

Q: What will you change in your life in anticipation of either a resurgence of this virus or possibly another unforeseen crisis?

A: We are now living with this pandemic. That is our new "normal". Things will never "go back" to the way they were, which so many people want. Health is wealth and we have to take better care of ourselves and be grateful for the little moments.

Max Isley

Owner

Hampton Kitchens

Q: In thinking of these last 90 or so days, tell us what you consider to be the most significant *Gear Switch*?

A: I went back to tapping the skill levels that each of us do best. The "cart was in the ditch" so I got out and went back to selling, the thing that I do best. The other folks here stepped into their strengths and said they would run that part and be fully accountable for it. We actually set up 2 scheduled Accountability calls each week and everyone had to make a commitment to what they would take responsibility for and by when, including me! I resisted but I am catching on and doing my part. It is all proving to create the bridge we need to get through this.

Q: What lessons did you learn?

A: I had a long talk with my younger brother whom I respect immensely and value as one of the greatest business minds I know. He challenged me to focus. Undeterred and without distraction. Laser focused on the most important thing I can do. I still get distracted and allow myself to get off tract, but I most always return quickly to my focus and #1 priority – going after new business and the "right kind". It is working. We have pushed cash flow projections out 2 more months from where they were.

Q: What will you change in your life in anticipation of either a resurgence of this virus or possibly another unforeseen crisis?

A: I am using this to prepare my staff for "*the new normal*". We are assuming this will be here for a while and we are adapting accordingly with our work ethic, our exposure to clients and their surroundings, our field people and how they need to operate and stay safe. We are using it as an opportunity to improve and inform. It is frustrating but not so much as losing business. It is just the way it is. We will do what is needed to survive and flourish. We can do this!!

Kathy MacKenzie
Director of Development
The Arts Club Theatre Company

Q: What is the Chrysalis? How did it come about?

A: When COVID-19 shut down our theatres in mid-March, we were exactly halfway through our season, with seven productions left to stage. We had sold nearly $4 million in ticket sales for the 2020 summer productions and we had announced our 2021 season and already sold more than 8 million in subscription sales.

In the days and weeks that followed, it became clear that we needed to S*witch Gears* to ensure the survival of the company. As production postponements became cancellations and the dozens of layoffs turned into hundreds of artists and staff being laid off, everyone turned to the fundraising department looking for a strategy to minimize the devastating loss to our charity. Based on previous experience at the Arts Club, finding $4 million was pretty unlikely. Normally, a successful fundraising campaign at the Arts Club could bring in $100,000, but that amount seemed insignificant compared to our dire need. Payroll alone was still over $50,000 per week. Initially, I set the stretch goal of raising a million dollars. And, thus was born the idea of the Chrysalis Campaign. We needed something dramatic that could inspire hope about the future. A few loyal donors, along with our Board, pooled their gifts to provide $100,000 in matching funds. This was an incentive offering to match all donations up to that amount. Messaging was key. We needed to know that we were in dire need while still conveying that we would endure and that a donation was an investment in the future. But the fundraising was not the only *Gear Switch* for the Arts Club. We knew that we needed to continue to engage our patrons and remain relevant. We quickly developed a weekly series called "Arts Club Artists Live from Home". Each week, we offered an honorarium to an artist whose contract at the Arts Club was cancelled and we asked them to tell a story, read a poem or do anything they liked and film it from home. At the same time, we also developed "Workshop Wednesdays" that provided live educational workshops about the theatre, for free, on ZOOM™, every Wednesday afternoon.

Q: How did it save the theatre from bankruptcy?

A: To date, over 500 donors have given and we are nearing $500,000 with one month left in the Campaign.

Q: Is this the future of the theatre?

A: Part of the process, for me, was accepting and grieving over the loss of what our theatre once was. I have come to realize that this virus will be with us for a long time. There will be some patrons who don't return. Our audiences tend to be older and we are known for our large blockbusters like "Kinky Boots" and "Sound of Music". However, in May 2020, the BC government declared that gatherings larger than 50 are prohibited until there is either a vaccine, treatment or herd immunity. Coming to terms with the fact that we will be unable to stage the kind of productions for which we have been celebrated is a hard pill to swallow. But I knew we had to find a way through it. If the arts sector couldn't find a creative solution, then who could?

Q: How will it affect the delivery of the production?

A: As it stands, our future will be an increased number of smaller productions. We are looking at multiple performances a day and, instead of 600+ patrons, there will be stage plays with one or two performers for an audience of 50, who will all sit two meters apart from those outside their households. We will also live stream these plays but whether there is an appetite to pay for online content remains to be seen.

Q: What lessons have you learned from this experience?

A: I've had to focus on a strategy for the future to get through the pandemic. I cannot be afraid to try new things. If they don't work, try something else. There are so many unknowns, I saw colleagues afraid to take any action at all.

Q: What have you discovered about yourself?

A: There have been highs and lows, but helping others through this has been rewarding. I have been working with other theatre companies across the country and sharing our success. As we have experienced our success, it has energized me to keep going and striving for more.

Q: In what ways did you *Switch Gears?*

A: Programming, messaging and fundraising all changed dramatically.

Q: What do you consider to be the most significant *Gear Switch*?

A: We exist to bring the community together and share the human experience. In the early days of this pandemic, it didn't feel like live theatre could exist in this environment. The biggest shift was accepting that we had to shift our business model and believe that we could be meaningful and serve our purpose in a new way.

Q: What wisdom can you share about *Switching Gears*?

A: Dream big. Inspire others. Stay hopeful and turn to others for support.

Carol Rossman

Artist

I am an artist who spends many hours a day in my home studio, particularly when preparing for a show. So staying at home with limited social events until the weekend is quite normal for me. Shortly after delivering a completed body of work to a museum, COVID-19 arrived. We were all confined to our homes. Oh, I thought to myself, preparing for my next show should be a breeze. No excuses to avoid working. I have all the time in the world. I might even get some household projects done with my husband. He, too, is now home. Imagine my shock and dismay, mixed with a little bit of shame, when I realized I just *Switched Gears* – from HIGH gear......to NEUTRAL. Not even LOW gear!!! After 3 months, I did get some studio work done, but not one single home project. No cleaned out drawers, no throwing out junk, no cataloguing our ceramics collection, no repairing our shower. And housekeeping

– my husband has been doing that, along with preparing most of our meals. Upon reflection, I've decided not to be too ashamed. I'm usually high energy, juggling many different responsibilities. I obviously needed to shut down for a while. My body said STOP! And so I did. I am now moving into LOW gear, on my way to a new CRUISE control.

Brody Todd

Junior Class

James Madison University

Q: In thinking of these last 90 or so days, tell us what you consider to be the most significant *Gear Switch*?

A: My most significant *Gear Switch* has been learning to adapt to completely virtual schooling. As a junior at JMU, I had become used to incredibly large, engaging, hands-on courses. It wasn't until the end of last spring, as the first lockdown began, that I had to figure out how to be successful in school when everything was online. Virtual classes technically fulfill the purpose of educating students; however I don't know how confidently I can say, "I'm being educated". The face-to-face version of education was how I felt I could best learn. The connection to my teachers and fellow students helped bestow confidence and I felt as if I was learning something new every time I went to class. With on-line instruction, I find myself having to self-teach most of the material in my courses, which has been a serious burden on me mentally and has caused me to feel much less successful and educated than before.

Q: What surprised you the most? What skills or experiences helped you navigate through the quarantine?

A: My biggest surprise was the realization that I had been taking many things in my life for granted. There were huge moments that I lost due to the pandemic, such as cancelled concerts and performances, family visits and vacations, plus more. However, what I really found myself missing the most were the little things – I miss little holiday parties with friends, seeing my professors on campus, and just being able to shake hands with new people. It seems the ability to personally connect with others was stripped from me, and that was more difficult to deal with than some of the seemingly bigger downfalls of the pandemic.

One of the main things that helped me navigate this quarantine was staying connected to close family and friends via on-line platforms. Early in the lockdown, I reconnected with a group of guys from my high school by playing video games together at night. Video games had not been a big part of my life pre-quarantine, but they became a way for me to feel connected to other people as I began to play with those guys. We talked about our struggles, what we missed, and helped give each other hope for the day when this is all over. This was a quick relief from the stress of living through it. Along the way, we rekindled our friendships and now we look forward to continuing those relationships in person when it is finally safe to do so. In a similar fashion, I reconnected with a lot of my family. I have not been good at calling or contacting my family using FaceTime™ on a regular basis, but I tried to find time to reach out not only to check on them, but to also give myself a chance to have someone to talk to and share what I was feeling during the quarantine. More than I want to see my friends, I can't wait for the day when I can see my whole family again.

Q: What lessons did you learn?

A: The pandemic taught me to never take a single thing for granted. As I mentioned before, I came to realize over the course of this year how much the little things in life meant to me, and also how little I appreciated them before they were gone. I can't wait for the day that I can return to a "normal" world again, and when that day comes, I am going to soak in everything that life has to offer and appreciate everything that I have.

Q: What new talents, creations or opportunities did you discover while dealing with the pandemic?

A: As a film student at JMU, I have learned a great deal regarding how to operate equipment, and how to shoot "technically sound" shots. These are obviously incredible important skills, but they don't allow for much creativity in my content creation. For this reason, I took the extra time that I was given during this pandemic to start learning everything I could about video editing. I have been able to teach myself so much about this art so that when we are past the Pandemic, I will be at the top of my class, and upon graduation, ready to take on the best roles that the entertainment industry has to offer.

Q: In what way did you *Switch Gears*?

A: During this pandemic, I *Switched Gears* by allowing myself to accept change. I don't like when things are unorganized, or change frequently, and this experience has been full of unexpected events. I struggled with this at first, but have learned to accept the changes that come with dealing with a deadly virus, and to appreciate the reasons behind everything rather than dwell on what I cannot control. This realization has relieved so much stress and has allowed me to work on what I can do in this moment, and look towards a brighter future at the end of this terribly difficult tunnel.

Q: What will you change in your life in anticipation of either a resurgence of this virus or possibly another unforeseen crisis?

A: In anticipation of another event similar to this virus, I would like to appreciate everything in my life just a little bit more. Whether it's something small or the most meaningful thing to me, I have learned that I miss it all the same now that so much has been taken away. If I am ever subjected to something similar to this crisis, I would like to be able to say that in the times before that event, I lived my life to the fullest, and had an immense amount of appreciation for everything that I had.

Q: What advice would you give a freshman entering JMU regarding the pandemic, dealing with COVID, and how to get the best out of their college experience?

A: My advice would be to drop any expectations. That's not to say that they shouldn't be excited about coming in, but rather have an open mind about what their experience will be. They may not get to attend the crazy frat parties or big football games, but that might lead them to join a smaller club or find a tight-knit group of friends that become their favorite part of college. This pandemic has definitely taken away a lot of fun aspects of college, but the time at JMU, or any other university, can still be the best years of your life if you make them so.

Matthew Manciagli

Owner

Fitness Center

"**When it rains, it pours**." I could sum up my entrepreneurial experience in 2020 with that one statement. Since the reopening of my fitness center, I've lost count of how many of my members have asked me, "How's the gym doing?" Before, the pandemic, that could have been taken a few ways. Now I know exactly what they are asking me – they want to know if I am going to survive. They want to know if I have plans of shutting my doors - permanently. They want to know if the loss of revenue is hurting me, putting the squeeze on every tightening situation. Since I was shut down for operation during a 2-month period (between March and June of 2020), nothing has felt the same. This year has been an emotional rollercoaster for me, and I would imagine it has been so for small business owners all over America. I say "American business owners," but I am well aware that I stand in solidarity with every small business owner around the world regardless of the industry we operate in.

For all the small business owners who are reading this, I know what you are going through, and I can relate to the confusion, frustration, anxiety, and uncertainly that every day brings. I hope that my words and story can bring, at the very least, a small bit of comfort in these troubled times. I can't promise that we will all survive this new reality, but I want you to understand that this was not your fault. This was an unforeseen situation that caught the world by surprise. Beating yourself up over this now will not change anything other than add another obstacle to an already challenging course.

Whether by unforeseen circumstances, or by enthusiastic volition, new entrepreneurs will be *Switching Gears* as their lives change drastically and rapidly – for better or for worse. For some entrepreneurs, it was a passion that motivated them to make the *Switch*. For others, it was out of necessity to provide for a family in a sluggish economy after losing a job, perhaps. Or maybe it was a spur-of-the-moment decision for the thrill seeker – the adventurer at heart. Regardless of the circumstances preceding the decision, the entrepreneurial leap is a leap like no other. Head first for some… feet first for others. My personal decision was made with both a genuine desire to help people achieve a healthier lifestyle, and, of course, to make money. Moreover, the prospect of setting my own path and work schedule was a motivating factor that has weighed heavily on my decision.

Alas, I was struck with visions of financial and personal freedom – the American Dream.

I started my fitness center in November of 2016. The construction of my franchise-based, 24-hour club started in the summer of that year, and I recall the day the contractor began the building process as extremely stressful. I knew that this was it. There was no turning back now. Alone, I kept tabs on the process, watching it through frequent visits with the contractor – making sure we were still on schedule. Once completed, again alone, I sat in an empty gym attempting to attract pre-sale prospects in hope of converting them to members (the first litmus test of my gym's ability to survive). Two months after my pre-sale period, my fitness equipment was delivered, and the next day I was officially in business. Without children of my own, I can only surmise that starting your first business is very similar to having your first child. You're excited, and yet terrified at the same time. You can read every book on entrepreneurship, craft a thorough budget, select the "perfect" location, and still....you can fail. You are hopeful and yet totally aware of the prospect of failure. The uncertainty can, for some, be unbearable, and for others, a rush – a grand shout of exultation. Regardless of the outcome, it is a courageous endeavor. That alone is worthy of admiration.

Unbeknownst to me at the time, my climb to profitability was long and arduous. The first lesson I learned as an entrepreneur was to get my "head out of the clouds." Entrepreneurship should never be approached with the "If you build it, they will come," mentality. That sentiment is best left for farm owners who build a baseball field and connect with ball-playing apparitions. Selling fitness memberships is trickier than it appears, and running a gym requires a great deal of attention and time. My assumption was that everyone wants to get healthy and fit, but it is sadly just not the case. Hell, I even gave away free one-year memberships to select individuals, and they showed up once or twice before never coming back in. Imagine that – I sell something that I can't give away for free! Nonetheless, I slowly built the membership up with the help of my family. My amazing wife, parents, and in-laws all played a pivotal role in helping me grow the business to financial stability right around January of 2020 – just months before the nationwide shutdown. Welcome to the new reality of living in the "Era of COVID-19."

Right around the beginning of March, I really started to panic; the writing was on the wall. What started as a whisper of a state shutdown soon became a shout of a proclamation as the Governor of Florida decided to temporarily relinquish business operations for non-essential business on March 20, 2020. I called my parents to let them know and to ask for their help in shutting the club down. My voice was shaking from the dread and anxiety of hearing the news. I was holding back tears, I won't lie. This felt like the end for me. The front door was locked, the A/C was set to 79 degrees, the music was turned off, and finally the lights. The lights where the last thing to be turned off. I recall the ominous echo of each breaker snapping to the "off position." My gym instantly felt distant to me – dead. I really didn't know if my business would survive beyond that point. Would I become a victim of circumstance; a casualty of a war-like situation against a microbial invader?

Through external events, I felt like my control of my business was futile. It feels like despair – hands and feet bound tight. You can't fight even if you want to. You are paralyzed, prostrated, and subject to the will of forces unknown. I want to be able to point to something I did as the reason I failed. Not like this. I did and still do my very best not to think about the financial ramifications. What I know is that I must keep doing something. Anything. This is a sink-or-swim situation, and I sure as hell was not going to drown without a good fight against this rising tide of uncertainty. Of course, you can tread water, but I would rather "Michael Phelps it" and kick my arms and feel like I'm going for the gold. Those who ride out the storm with wishful thinking may find their business in a relentless undertow – those who fight the turbulence to keep their heads above water at least a little longer.

The fight-or-flight response became the greatest instigator of my *Shifting Gears*. As mentioned, responding to this situation doesn't guarantee success, but by not responding, you most certainly increase your chances of failure. As Louis Pasteur said, "Chance favors the prepared mind." For many small business owners, the status quo simply will not work moving forward. New times call for new changes, innovations, and the ability to adapt to an ever-evolving business landscape. Each industry has unique challenges that must be met, but first and foremost, we all have to think about keeping our customers safe and healthy. And here begins the innovative process of business survival.

Lesson 1:

Focus on what you can control. The first step I made in my attempt to keep my business afloat was to organize my thoughts around all the elements of my business over which I still had control. Paying little attention to the external environment, I realized that I had control over the cleanliness of my club, its atmosphere and my connection to my members through social media. As the owner of a franchise, there are plenty of rules and regulations that stifle immediate action and innovation but working within my limitations, I had decided on three goals for my club during the shutdown. #1 was to find new ways of keeping my members safe during the pandemic. #2 was to make some simple updates to my club's décor to "wow" my members when they came back. And #3 was to increase my use of social media to connect to my members. That's where I felt I could make the biggest impact to my business while being able to accomplish these goals cost effectively and time efficiently. You don't have to do something big and grand to make an impact; you want to show your clients that you simply care about them. That really means more to people than you know.

Before the pandemic, I had community towels on my machines that I would change out regularly. I knew that this would not work in a post-pandemic world so I simply ordered about 200 microfiber mini towels. As an added touch, I order a massive pack of 1-inch "Thank You" stickers and white & black currency bands. I rolled the towels, wrapped them in a currency band, and placed a sticker on the band to hold the towel securely wrapped. When the club re-opened, it was a hit with my members. Cost effectively, I had added value to my members' experience and created a safer environment by offering individual towels. Simple! I killed two birds with one stone. It took a little creativity, and some searching on Amazon, but I found a solution to a challenge. I have continued this practice and will continue to do so. This is one example of a simple change I made as I went along the way. It helped me to not only retain members, but attract some new ones in the process. Additionally, some new cleaning protocols were implemented to further the safety of my members. In my industry, gym cleanliness is make-or-break, especially in a post-COVID environment.

Despite my lack of enthusiasm for social media, I made brilliant use of it during the shutdown. This helped me to stay connected to my members and keep them informed of any relevant information regarding my club's reopening. Moreover, it gave me an opportunity to simply say "Thank You" to all my members for being both loyal to my club and patient during our closure. Again, I was amazed to find how much my members appreciated the simple gesture of hearing "Thank You." As with the changes to my cleaning protocol, I felt in control of the communication I had with the members. I embraced this so much that, within 2 days, I built a simple website to give my members guidance for at home workouts. This is a solid example of something I would not have considered without the pandemic providing a challenge to overcome. Moving swiftly to a digital platform to stay in touch with and keep my members active at home created a potential future opportunity for an extension business. With a little creativity and swift action, I used what control I had over my communication to again, build value for my members. Even if it had only impacted one person, it was worth it.

My wife had always told me that one thing my club lacked was décor that best matched me and my personality. She was a great source to pull from when coming up with ideas for some décor changes. It didn't take me long to sketch some ideas as to what my club should feel like – how I wanted to better represent my attitude and tastes. I love the feel of a wilderness lodge – the wood, the rawness and the brawn associated with its construction. Rustic and historic in its feel is an atmosphere that, for me, evokes both a sense of calm and appreciation for hard work. It conjures up images of flannel-wearing, boot-kicking, hard-working, men and women, up early in the morning to meet the day with an axe-wielding vigor. That's me…..a lumberjack of my trade. A beard-sporting, work-ethic minded owner who loves to exercise and loves the woods!

As a franchise owner, there were many restrictions as to what I could do regarding the modification of my club. I had to get really creative in designing a custom décor that would both make my club stand out and remain in compliance with the rules. This would lead me into the second lesson – pool your personal resources.

Lesson 2

Draw from your talents. With little to no business income, I had to be very careful in how I spent money redesigning my club's atmosphere. To reduce cost, I used my recently acquired talent of woodworking to be my greatest resource. I would have never imagined that I would actually use this hobby-related skill in such a profound way, but it was a talent, and I was going to get the most out of it. Fortunately for me, much of what I wanted to do from a décor perspective was wood oriented, but everything I was about to build was absolutely foreign to me. I was planning on building some rather large table-like structures, complex wall décor, and custom chandeliers, none of which I ever made before. Uncorrupted by any strict techniques, I set to simply design these items as I felt best. No rules, just some will power, and a "can-do" attitude. For me, this brought out some of my most creative moments yet. For almost a whole month, I was at my club working alone with nothing but some cold beer, my tools, and Bob Dylan for some audible stimulation. I was propelled, into a project that started with a single cut of wood and ended with the atmosphere I set out to create. It may, to date, be one of the most revered accomplishments of my life. I fashioned, from both wood and imagination, functional, aesthetically pleasing furnishings that added so much life and personality to my club. I was proud….. really proud. This pandemic had brought about a sharpening of a recently acquired skill. Not only did I enhance my club, I am a better woodworker for doing so. We all have talents that can be utilized for our businesses' benefit during this pandemic. Whether that talent is artistic, creative, intellectual, or otherwise – you need to really give your talents a long, hard look and see how they can be used to make positive impacts.

Lesson 3

Learn to be comfortable with failure.

I made a reference to this early on, but I feel like it has to be said again – the negative results of this pandemic are not your fault. It's simply a fact that many of our businesses will not survive the pandemic, and you have to start being comfortable with that. My club has been open for the past 5 months, and I still don't know if I am going to survive. All I could do was control whatever I could within my power, and if it fails, at least I know that I tried my best. I didn't ask for this and neither did you. It is what it is. However, let me put this suggestion out there for you – this may be an opportunity to *Switch Gears into* a new career path. I think that it's a great time to really sit down and reassess where you are in life and if what you have done to this point has really made you happy. There is so much to learn, and accessing knowledge cost-effectively via the web is growing easier every day. *Switching Gears* doesn't necessarily relate to you and your career/small business at present; it could relate to entirely new pathways in life. I always make it a point to learn something new each day. It keeps my options open and allows me to explore the potential. What matters now is that you find a bridge – a plan – to get you from where you are now to where you want to be in the future. If you don't see a path forward with your current small business, start working on a new plan. If you are truly passionate about your small business, get creative and push the envelope a little… carve out your niche.

There is always a success around every failure. Read any successful business owner's story and you will be amazed at how many times they failed before they became successful. It's a natural part of the process. What you need to do is learn from each failure. How can you do it better next time? The bottom line is – do not let a negative outcome destroy you. It's not worth letting that happen. Find the silver lining and start a new chapter in life. A better chapter. *Switch* those *Gears* as many times as necessary to find the right *Gear*. Then just cruise and enjoy life.

A final thought:

This writing was primarily directed to small business owners, but the underlying concept applies to any and every one. It's not just small business owners who are hurting. As the economy is altered, many people will lose their jobs and as a result they, too, will be forced to *Switch Gears*. The best advice I can give is to plan a course of action and act on it. If you take anything away from this, please remember that you must "keep on keeping on"! The "deer in the headlights" move is one that only ends one way. Do what you can. Work on what you can control. Be resourceful. Get out of your comfort zone – it won't ever be easy, but I truly believe that we all have it in us to overcome this pandemic, both mentally and financially. To those who are still employed and/or financially stable, please support your local businesses. We all need you more today than ever before. In the day of online business, it's easy to forget that there are hardworking families in your community who have worked hard to pursue the dream of entrepreneurship. Please be cognizant of their existence and support them in any way you can. I feel comfortable in speaking for all small business owners when I say "THANK YOU". Thank you for helping us remain relevant in a digital world. A main street without local, small storefronts is an image which I couldn't bear. For when we reach a reality like that, we have lost the heart of capitalism, and we will have dowsed the flames of <u>The American Dream.</u>

12
ATTRIBUTES

———————

Many attributes became apparent to us as we listened to these stories. For each person, some attributes were already honed before the *Switch* and others were learned as a result of the process of *Switching* **Gears**.

13
SUMMARY & CONCLUSION

If you are struggling with the idea of facing a transition in life or "retiring", this book can offer you an opportunity to explore your notions, thoughts and feelings with regard to how you will make that *Gear Switch* – to help you learn how you undergo a process of change or a period of transition. There are three basic questions to ponder as you begin:

1. What is my life's purpose as I transition in life?
2. Identify and list either your core competencies, skills or abilities. Examples might be interpersonal processing, or creative thinking.....
3. How might all of your skills and strengths help you successfully achieve your Purpose in life or do they act as an obstacle or detriment?

We aren't sure what else we can add to the stories in *Switching Gears.* There are those of you who haven't been successful at Switching *Gears,* and those who are stuck in the past, reliving it and hoping it will change. You must understand that if you have *Switched Gears* and are stuck in **neutral**, without you moving the needle, nothing is going to happen.

For all the stories in this book, there are many more that we haven't told. We would love to read yours and possibly share in our next book. *Switching Gears* in today's world is critical for learning to adapt, to change and transition into something or someone who hasn't existed before but perhaps wanted to. This book has been a major part of our life for the last three to four years. Everywhere we go, everyone we meet is intrigued with our title and the meaning of *Switching Gears*.

A quote from <u>Politico</u> sums up these times and is so apt for our book:

> *"It's clear that in a crisis, the "rules don't apply" – which makes you wonder why there are rules in the first place. This is an unprecedented opportunity to not just hit the pause button and temporarily ease the pain but to permanently change the rules so that untold millions of people aren't so vulnerable to begin with."*

For our next book, tell us your story about your *Switching Gears* experience and what either enabled you to be successful or, if you failed, why. We want to share stories of readers who have validated their meaning of successfully *Switching Gears* as well as the obstacles that prevented success. Every story can be a learning experience for others.

Switching Gears is about life's transitions. Its purpose is to help the reader explore its meaning through real life stories and to ponder questions such as "Who am I? What do I want? Where am I going? How am I going to get there?"

Think about Robert Frost "***The Road Not Taken***" – Two roads diverged in a yellow wood, and I took the one less travelled – that has made all the difference.

This book contains inspiring stories from real people as they confront and adjust to the roadblocks of life and then overcome those obstacles by life-altering challenges.

Switching Gears puts the reader in the drivers seat heading to new beginnings and provides lessons in living by helping people open their eyes and hearts to a myriad of possibilities.

> *"Switching Gears speaks to two of the most important qualities for a successful life – adaptability and resilience. Pour your favorite beverage, sit back, and read true life stories of people who have risen above the most difficult challenges. You will gain inspiring insights and ideas for successfully navigating this rapidly changing world."*

- David McNally,

Bestselling Author, "Even Eagles Need A Push" and "Be Your Own Brand"

The secret of change is to focus all of our energy not on fighting the old, but on building the new.

Socrates